Klett Wortschatz

AF203599

Idiomatic English in context

Sicher im Ausdruck

von Louise Carleton-Gertsch

Ernst Klett Sprachen
Stuttgart

Idiomatic English in context

Sicher im Ausdruck

von Louise Carleton-Gertsch

Beratende Mitarbeit: Uli Nürnberger

Bildquellen

www.cartoonstock.com, Lansdown Mews, Bath, Avon:
pp. 72 (Bryant, Adey), 94 (kes), 109 (Wildt, Chris), 112 (Schwadron, Harley),
113 (Goddard, Clive), 128 (Reynolds, Dan), 162 (Naf), 165.1 (Morris, John),
165.2 (Fran), 183 (Shapiro, Mike), 195 (Wildt, Chris), 199 (Goddard, Clive)
Businesscartoons Visual Humour, Stockton-on-Tees:
pp. 120, 141, 154, 186, 188 (Morris, John)

Nicht in allen Fällen war es uns möglich, den uns namentlich bekannten
Rechteinhaber ausfindig zu machen. Berechtigte Ansprüche werden
selbstverständlich im Rahmen der branchenüblichen Vereinbarungen
abgegolten.

1. Auflage   1 12 11 10 9 | 2025 24 23 22

Alle Drucke dieser Auflage sind untereinander unverändert und können
im Unterricht nebeneinander verwendet werden.
Die letzte Zahl bezeichnet das Jahr dieses Druckes.

© Ernst Klett Sprachen GmbH, Rotebühlstr. 77, 70178 Stuttgart, 2008.
Alle Rechte vorbehalten.
Das Werk und seine Teile sind urheberrechtlich geschützt. Jede Nutzung
in anderen als den gesetzlich zugelassenen Fällen bedarf der vorherigen
schriftlichen Einwilligung des Verlages.

Internetadresse: www.klett-sprachen.de
Redaktion: Don Haupt
Druck: Elanders GmbH, Waiblingen

Printed in Germany
ISBN 978-3-12-519950-7

All about people

Living together

Global issues

Work and leisure

Film, fashion and the media

Literature and the arts

Study points

When you learn a foreign language such as English, you need to learn vocabulary so that you can talk about different topics. However, you will soon find that this is not enough. If you want to improve your English, you will also need to learn collocations (words which commonly go together) and idiomatic expressions. This will not only help you to increase your vocabulary but will also enable you to sound more natural and improve your style. In addition, if you can avoid making common mistakes, especially where there is the risk of interference from German, you will sound more like a native speaker.

Idiomatic English in context deals with these broader aspects of language learning. Single lexical items are covered in *Words in context* so as a rule they are not explained in this book. In order to be able to cover some areas in greater depth, *Idiomatic English in context* is divided into two sections: **Topics** and **Study points**.

Topics

This section is divided into six different chapters. Each chapter contains a variety of texts that put collocations, set phrases and idioms in different thematic contexts. The texts are very diverse, including dialogues, extracts from discussions, news broadcasts, advertising texts, informative texts, quizzes and speeches.

The expressions to be learned have been highlighted in colour (e.g. **at the age of**). These expressions are repeated on the right-hand side and translated into German. Additional explanations and tips on usage are also given. You will need to look closely for the expressions on the right-hand page because they are arranged in three different categories, and not simply listed as they occur in the text. This will help you to learn the items more easily. The categories are always in the following order:
- "Talking about" boxes which contain expressions concerning a particular word or subject
- idioms and collocations
- "Be careful", which includes false friends and expressions which are similar to but not the same as the German equivalents.

After some entries you will see a page number in colour (e.g. **p. 164**). This refers you to a particular page in the Study points (or in a few cases you will be directed to a "Talking about" box in another section of Topics) where you will find more information on this point.

Sometimes phrasal verbs in the texts have been marked in **bold** (e.g. **leave off**). An exercise on the same page will help you to work out their meanings. Phrasal verbs marked with an asterisk are informal.

At the end of each chapter there are four pages of exercises so that you can see how much you have learnt.

Study points

This section focuses on certain areas that can be problematic for German speakers of English. The Study points will not only enable you to improve your written language (including help with easily confused words, overused words, prepositions, alternatives for phrasal verbs, tips for writing essays and presentations) but will also help you to improve your spoken English and comprehension skills (such as choosing the right register, understanding euphemisms, paraphrasing and conversational responses).

The Study points do not contain endless lists of expressions. We have selected some of the more common ones because it is better to learn a few and to be able to use them correctly. In most cases there is an explanatory text on the left-hand page and exercises on the right-hand side. The latter enable you to practise what you have just read.

The answers to all of the exercises as well as the quizzes in the text can be found in the "Key to the exercises" at the back of the book (from page 200 onwards).

Abbreviations and symbols used

AE	American English	*	informal
BE	British English	!	false friend
fig.	figurative	=	synonym
inf.	informal	≠	opposite
o.s.	oneself		
p.	page		
s.o.	someone		
s.th.	something		
usu.	usually		

Family ties

In 1999 *Time Magazine* published the "Time 100", a list of the 100 most important people in the twentieth century. Some of them are described below. Do you know who they are?

1. The head of this famous **family** was **descended from** Irish-Americans. Politics **ran in the family**. There was undoubtedly **sibling rivalry** between the nine children although the family was very **close-knit**. One of the sons became the youngest US president ever. Following his assassination, two of his brothers **followed in his footsteps** – also both running for the presidency. Members of the **extended family** are still involved in US politics to this day.

2. This famous US actress spent much of her childhood in foster homes. After working as a photographer's model she made her first film in 1948 and achieved stardom as a blonde sex symbol a few years later. Her private life, including three **failed marriages**, was widely publicized. She **died from** a drug overdose. It is uncertain whether it was an accident or whether she **committed suicide**.

3. This person was born into an English aristocratic family and married into royalty. Over the next few years she **gave birth to** two sons then separated from her husband. The marriage **ended in divorce**. She became well-known for her support of charity projects. Her life was tragically **cut short** – she died in a car accident when she was only 36. Many people reacted as if they had lost their **own flesh and blood**. Her sons are now continuing some of the charity work started by their **late mother**.

4. This Scot had a large **immediate family** – he had eight siblings and half-siblings. His father **passed away** when he was 14, and he then moved to London where he later studied medicine. In 1928 he accidentally made a discovery which was to change the way bacterial infections are treated. He was awarded the Nobel Prize for medicine in 1945.

5. She was born in Macedonia in 1910 to a family of Albanian descent. **At the age of** 18 she joined a community of Irish nuns and moved to Calcutta. In 1950 she founded her own order, devoted to helping the poorest of the poor. She lived to a **ripe old age**.

Answers: p. 200

Talking about families

A family might be	loving	*liebevoll*
	close-knit [nɪt] / close	*eng*
	dysfunctional	*gestört*

extended family	*Großfamilie*
immediate / close **family**	*engste Familie*

Talking about death

People will often avoid saying "X has died". They prefer to use euphemisms. Two of the most common are "X has **passed away**" and "X has passed on". You might also hear different idioms. Whilst it is important that you understand them, it is better not to use them to avoid upsetting anyone. Here are some humorous, informal idioms: "X has kicked the bucket", "X has popped his clogs", "X has bitten the dust".
The person who has died is referred to as "the deceased".
When someone informs you that a relation or friend has died, you can say "My condolences" or "My sympathies".

p. 164

family ties	*Familienbande*
to be descended from	*abstammen von*
to run in the family *(idiom)*	*in der Familie liegen*
sibling rivalry ['raɪvlrɪ]	*Rivalität unter Geschwistern*

The word "sibling" is rather formal. If you are talking to friends, it is more usual to talk about "brothers and sisters" rather than "siblings".

to follow in s.o.'s footsteps *(idiom)*	*in jds. Fußstapfen treten*
failed marriage	*gescheiterte Ehe*
to commit suicide	*Selbstmord begehen*
to give birth to (a son / daughter)	*(einen Sohn / eine Tochter) auf die Welt bringen*
to end in divorce [dɪ'vɔːs]	*geschieden werden*

A marriage "ends in divorce", a couple "gets a divorce" or "divorces" and one person "divorces" another person.

to cut s.th. short	*etw. vorzeitig beenden*

A common idiom is "to cut a long story short" *(um es kurz zu machen)*.

one's own flesh and blood *(idiom)*	*sein eigen Fleisch und Blut*
to live to a ripe old age *(idiom)*	*ein hohes Alter erreichen*

the Smith family / the Smiths	*die Familie Smith*

Remember, don't use the German word order!

to die <u>from</u> an overdose	*an einer Überdosis sterben*
to die <u>of</u> an illness	*an einer Krankheit sterben*

When the adjective "late" is used before a noun, the meaning is "dead", e.g. "**late mother**" *(verstorbene Mutter)*.

<u>at</u> the age of	*im Alter von*

Love is in the air

Three romantic comedies

The Break-Up starts where most other romantic comedies **leave off**: after a boy and girl have **fallen in love** and moved in together to live **happily ever after** … right when Brooke **dumps** her boyfriend Gary. But neither of them wants to leave their shared home. What follows is a battle of the sexes with **blind dates**, parties and broken promises.

Love Actually explores the ups and downs of eight relationships in the weeks before Christmas. The couples involved include the Prime Minister, who's **infatuated with** a member of his staff; a widower whose young son has a schoolboy **crush** and a writer who **falls for** his Portuguese housekeeper …

4 Weddings and a Funeral **follows the fortunes** of **confirmed bachelor** Charles and his **single** friends as they wonder if they will ever find true love and **tie the knot**.

Girl talk

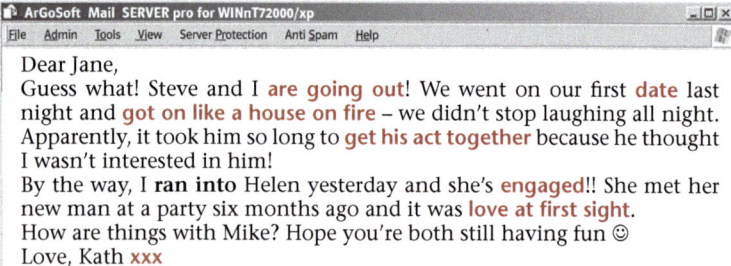

Dear Jane,
Guess what! Steve and I **are going out**! We went on our first **date** last night and **got on like a house on fire** – we didn't stop laughing all night. Apparently, it took him so long to **get his act together** because he thought I wasn't interested in him!
By the way, I **ran into** Helen yesterday and she's **engaged**!! She met her new man at a party six months ago and it was **love at first sight**.
How are things with Mike? Hope you're both still having fun ☺
Love, Kath **xxx**

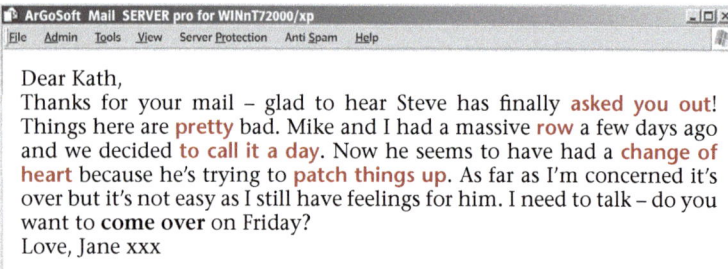

Dear Kath,
Thanks for your mail – glad to hear Steve has finally **asked you out**! Things here are **pretty** bad. Mike and I had a massive **row** a few days ago and we decided **to call it a day**. Now he seems to have had a **change of heart** because he's trying to **patch things up**. As far as I'm concerned it's over but it's not easy as I still have feelings for him. I need to talk – do you want to **come over** on Friday?
Love, Jane xxx

Which expression means the same as these phrasal verbs?

1. *to leave off	a) to visit s.o. at his / her house
2. to run into s.o.	b) to finish
3. to come over	c) to meet s.o. unexpectedly

Talking about relationships

break-up	*Trennung*
to love s.o.	to be attracted to s.o.
	to fancy s.o. *(inf.)*
	to have a crush (on s.o.) *(inf.)*
	to fall for s.o.
	to fall (madly) in love with s.o. *(idiom)*
	to be head over heels in love with s.o. *(inf., idiom)*
	to be infatuated [ɪnˈfætjʊeɪtɪd] **with s.o.**
to end a relationship	**to dump s.o.** *(inf.)*
(if one person does so)	to walk out on s.o. *(inf.)*
	to break up with s.o.
	to split up with s.o.
to end a relationship	**to break up** / to split up
(if both partners do so)	to separate [ˈsepəreɪt]
	to go separate [ˈseprət] ways
	to call it a day *(inf., idiom)*

The phrase "and they all lived **happily ever after**" is a set phrase which you often read at the end of fairy stories.

(to go on a) **blind date** *(idiom)*	*eine Verabredung mit einer / einem Unbekannten (haben)*
The film follows the fortunes of ...	*Der Film erzählt die Geschichte von ...*
confirmed bachelor [ˈbætʃələ]	*eingefleischter Junggeselle*
to tie the knot (with s.o.) *(inf., idiom)*	*(jdn.) heiraten*
to go out with s.o. *(BE)* = to date s.o. *(AE)*	*mit jdm. (aus)gehen*
to go on a date with s.o.	*ein Rendezvous mit jdm. haben*
to get on like a house on fire *(inf., idiom)*	*sich blendend verstehen*
to get one's act together *(inf., idiom)*	*die Kurve kriegen*
to ask s.o. out	*jdn. zu einem Rendezvous einladen*
to have a row [raʊ] **(with s.o.)** *(inf.)*	*sich (mit jdm.) streiten*
to have a change of heart *(idiom)*	*seine Meinung ändern*
to patch things up *(inf.)*	*einen Streit beilegen*

"**Single**" is an adjective and usually comes before a noun. The German word "*Single*" is translated as "single person", also as "singleton" *(inf.)*.

engaged (to be married) !	*verlobt*	p. 131
love <u>at</u> first sight *(idiom)*	*Liebe auf den ersten Blick*	p. 136

If someone signs off a letter, mail or message with "**xxx**", they represent kisses. "ooo" means hugs.

In informal English the word "**pretty**" is used instead of the more formal "fairly" or "rather". p. 186

Conversations overheard in a bar

What's up? You've been in a really foul mood all day!

I've had it up to here right now! I've been busting a gut trying to get this bloody report finished and Sue seems to take it all for granted. And then she came in today and blamed me for not having finished the presentation. I'm just sick and tired of it! It's always the same old story …

I'm beginning to have second thoughts about going to Spain.

You're kidding! You'll have such a good time when you're there.

I suppose so. It's just my gut feeling isn't really right.

That e-mail you sent really made my day!

Yeah, mine too. I was feeling a bit low and it really cheered me up.

I was in fits when I read it, especially the bit about the dog.

Her SMS threw me completely. I didn't know she was thinking of leaving.

Well she's been a bit down in the dumps recently and I think what happened on Monday was simply the last straw. Apparently she's been toying with the idea for some time now.

Have you seen Jane today? She was over the moon when I told her about the tickets.

I know. I met her on the way here and she can't wait to go.

Talking about feelings

to be depressed	**to feel low** *(inf.)*
	to feel blue *(inf.)*
	to be down in the dumps *(inf., idiom)*
to be very happy / to be ecstatic	**to be over the moon (about s.th.)** *(inf., idiom)*
	to be floating / walking on air *(idiom)*
	to be on cloud nine *(inf., idiom)*

What's up? *(inf., idiom)*	*Was gibt's? / Was ist los?*
to be in a foul mood	*mies gelaunt sein*
I've had it (up to here). *(inf., idiom)*	*Es steht mir bis oben hin.*
to bust a gut *(inf., idiom)*	*sich ein Bein ausreißen*
to take s.th. for granted *(idiom)*	*etw. für selbstverständlich halten*
to be sick and tired of s.th. *(inf., idiom)*	*etw. grundsätzlich satthaben*

The order of the words in the expression "**sick and tired**" cannot be changed. There are other similar expressions which are made up of two words joined by a conjunction (usually "and"), e.g.

peace and quiet	*Ruhe und Frieden*
odds and ends	*Kleinkram*
here and there	*hier und da*
down and out	*heruntergekommen*

It's always the same old story!	*Es ist immer das gleiche Lied!*
to have second thoughts about (doing) s.th. *(idiom)*	*an etw. zweifeln, es sich anders überlegen*
You're kidding! *(inf.)*	*Das ist ein Scherz!*
gut feeling *(idiom)*	*Bauchgefühl*
to make s.o.'s day	*jds. Tag retten*
to be in fits (of laughter)	*sich kaputtlachen*
to throw s.o. *(inf.)*	*jdn. durcheinanderbringen*
to be the last (*also* final) **straw** *(idiom)*	*das Fass zum Überlaufen bringen*
to toy with an idea	*mit einem Gedanken spielen*

The expression "**to overhear**" means *zufällig mithören*. It has nothing to do with the German expression *überhören*. This is translated as "to not hear", e.g. "I did not hear my alarm clock.". If you mean not wanting to hear, then you could also say "to ignore", e.g. "She ignored his remark about her hair.".

"**Bloody**" is a medium to strong swear word used in British English. You will often hear it used as an adjective to intensify a noun, e.g. "bloody report", or in exclamations such as "bloody hell". You should avoid using swear words in English, especially in writing, as they might cause offence. p. 174

to blame s.o. <u>for</u> s.th. !	*jdm. die Schuld an etw. geben*	p. 130

Writing a story – creating a main character

Your main character **is at the heart of** your story. **For the sake of simplicity** let us imagine it is a male figure. Your task is to **bring him to life** and to make him memorable. Here are a few tips to get you started.

Begin by writing down a few general points such as age, appearance and what he does. Even his name might be helpful at this stage. Now consider the following:

What is his character like? Does he **have both feet on the ground** or is his **head in the clouds**? Does he **have a good sense of humour**? Is he **set in his ways**? Does he ever **let his hair down**?

How does he react in certain situations? Does he **get worked up about** things easily?

How does he **get on with** others? Does he **keep himself to himself**? Does he **rub people up the wrong way**? Does he dominate the conversation and talk **nineteen to the dozen**?

What does he look like? Is he well-dressed or perhaps a little **down-at-heel**?

How does he behave in certain situations, i.e. does he have any nervous habits? Does he **bite his nails** when he is nervous? Does he **run his fingers through his hair** when he is deep in thought? Or perhaps he starts **drumming his fingers** on the table when he gets **irritated**.

What are his strengths and weaknesses? Does he have any burning ambitions?

Remember your character must be **human**, which means he shouldn't be perfect! Even if he has a **heart of gold**, he should have at least one weakness. Otherwise he runs the risk of being a **dead bore** and the reader will not **believe in him**.

Talking about nervous habits

to bite one's nails	*an den Nägeln kauen*
to run one's fingers through one's hair	*sich mit den Fingern durch die Haare fahren*
to drum one's fingers on the table	*mit den Fingern auf den Tisch trommeln*
to grind [aɪ] one's teeth	*mit den Zähnen knirschen*
to pick one's nose	*in der Nase bohren*
to clench one's fist	*eine Faust machen*
to furrow one's brow [braʊ]	*die Stirn runzeln*
to be at the heart of s.th.	*im Mittelpunkt stehen*

This expression is used to talk about the most important part of something, e.g. "Creating more jobs is at the heart of their plan.".

for the sake of simplicity	*der Einfachheit halber*
to bring s.o. to life	*jdn. zum Leben erwecken*
to have both feet on the ground *(idiom)*	*mit beiden Beinen (fest) im Leben stehen*
to have one's head in the clouds *(idiom)*	*mit seinen Gedanken ganz woanders sein*
to be set in one's ways	*in seinen Gewohnheiten festgefahren sein*
to let one's hair down *(idiom)*	*sich gehen lassen*
to get worked up about s.th.	*sich über etw. aufregen*
to get on with s.o.	*sich mit jdm. verstehen*
to keep o.s. to o.s. *(idiom)*	*für sich allein bleiben*
to rub s.o. up the wrong way *(idiom)*	*bei jdm. anecken*
to talk nineteen to the dozen *(inf., idiom)*	*reden wie ein Wasserfall*
down-at-heel *(idiom)*	*heruntergekommen*
to have a heart of gold *(idiom)*	*ein herzensguter Mensch sein*
to have a good sense <u>of</u> humour	*einen guten Sinn für Humor haben*
irritated !	*verärgert*
human !	*menschlich*

In informal English the word **"dead"** is used instead of the more formal "extremely" or "very", so a **"dead bore"** is someone who is extremely boring *(ein furchtbarer Langweiler)*.

p. 186

to believe <u>in</u> s.o.	*an jdn. glauben*

The common cold

You'll probably catch more colds in your lifetime than any other kind of illness. This is partly because they are **passed on** quickly – people often **pick up** the virus by touching something with cold germs on it or by inhaling cold germs. Colds tend to **go round** more in the winter months.

If you have a runny nose or sore throat, a headache and generally feel a bit under the weather, you might well be going down with a cold. Although there is no cure, rest and drinking lots of fluids will help your body to **fight off** the virus and to **get over** it more quickly. Over-the-counter cold remedies might also help. Your symptoms should **clear up** within a week and you'll soon be back on your feet again.

Find the expression on the right which means the same as each phrasal verb on the left.	
1. to pass s.th. on	a) to recover from s.th.
2. *to pick s.th. up	b) to improve
3. to go round (also: around)	c) to catch s.th.
4. to fight s.th. off	d) to transmit s.th.
5. to get over s.th.	e) to circulate
6. to clear up	f) to prevent s.th. making you ill

Notices in the waiting room

●
We provide nursing care for sick children and adults of all ages in their own homes. This can include care for people who have a long-term illness, those recovering from an operation and for terminally ill patients. Contact this number for further information: 0208 996 4394.

●
Our surgery will be closed for two weeks in July. If your medication or tablets are going to run out during this period, please ask the doctor for a new prescription.

●
Are you allergic to pollen? Do you suffer from hay fever? Make an appointment with the doctor for a free allergy test.

Talking about getting ill

to catch a cold	*sich erkälten*
to contract (a disease)	*an etw. erkranken*
to develop cancer	*an Krebs erkranken*
to pick up a bug *(inf.)*	*sich etw. einfangen*
to fall ill / to be taken ill	*krank werden*
to go down with s.th. *(inf.)*	*an etw. erkranken*

This phrase is often used in the present progressive or in the present perfect:
"He's going down with a cold." / "He's gone down with a cold."
With "I" you use "come" instead of "go":
"I am coming down with a cold." / "I have come down with a cold."

Talking about feeling ill

I don't feel very well / I feel unwell	**I feel a bit under the weather** *(inf., idiom)*
	I feel a bit off-colour *(inf., idiom)*
	I feel a bit run down
I'm getting better	I'm on the mend *(inf., idiom)*
	I'm recovering (from s.th.)
I'm better	**I'm back on my feet (again)** *(inf.)*
	I'm fighting fit *(inf., idiom)*

runny nose	*laufende Nase*
≠ blocked (up) nose	*verstopfte Nase*
sore throat	*Halsschmerzen*
over-the-counter	*rezeptfrei*
= without a prescription	
terminally ill	*todkrank*
seriously ill	*ernsthaft krank*

sick	*krank*

"Sick" is used before a noun, but "ill" is used after a noun:
"He is looking after his sick mother. She is very ill."
"Ill" may be used before a noun if qualified by an adverb, e.g. "a terminally ill patient". p. 126

to be sick	*sich übergeben*
I feel sick	*mir ist übel*
to be ill	*krank sein*

BE and *AE:* Unlike the British, the Americans use the word "sick" to mean someone is ill and does not feel well.

surgery = doctor's surgery	*Arztpraxis*	
tablet = pill **!**	*Tablette*	p. 131
prescription	*Rezept*	p. 132
to be allergic <u>to</u> s.th.	*allergisch gegen etw. sein*	
to suffer <u>from</u> s.th	*unter etw. leiden*	
appointment	*Termin*	p. 118

How do you feel today?

Doctor: Good morning, Mr Tate. Please take a seat. Now what can I do for you?

Mr Tate: Well, I go running a couple of times a week and I thought I was **in** pretty **good shape**. But I was out yesterday and I **hurt** my leg – I think I pulled a muscle.

Doctor: Let me have a look ... Hm, it's a little swollen. Rest it for a few days and don't put any pressure on it. Take a painkiller to **ease the pain**. You should be back on your feet again in a couple of days. But remember to **take it easy** when you start running again and don't overdo it!

Doctor: Hello **Ms** Day. So what seems to be the trouble?

Ms Day: I've had a **splitting headache** since yesterday and I've **got a temperature**. I'm **aching** all over and I feel really run down. **The thing is,** I've got to **be back on form** next week as I'm going on holiday. What can I do?

Doctor: You've got the flu. You need to go to bed, get plenty of rest and drink lots of fluids. I'll write you a prescription for some painkillers – take one every six hours. You should be over the worst by the weekend. **Get well soon** and enjoy your holiday!

Road accident – A41 closed

A **fatal** accident closed the A41 in both directions this morning. At 7.52 a.m. a lorry drove through a red light and crashed into a car. The car driver **sustained major head injuries**. Both he and the two passengers were taken by **ambulance** to the accident and emergency department at Watford General Hospital. The driver **died from his injuries** on arrival. According to doctors the front passenger's life is **hanging in the balance** and it is not known whether she will **pull through**. The other passenger's condition is also said to be **critical**. The lorry driver was not seriously **injured** – he **got away** with a few **cuts and bruises**. The police are appealing for anyone who witnessed the accident to **come forward**.

Which expression means the same as each of the phrasal verbs?

1. to pull through	*a) to offer help or information*
2. to get away with s.th.	*b) to survive*
3. to come forward	*c) to escape*

Talking about how you are	
to be in good shape	*fit sein*
≠ to be in bad shape	
to be back on form	*wieder in Form sein*

Talking about pain

In English the two verbs "**ache**" and "**hurt**" have different meanings. If a part of your body "aches", then you have a continuous pain which is usually not very strong. If it "hurts", it is normally a pain that has been caused by an injury, e.g. "My leg aches." but "My leg hurts where I banged it against the table.".
A "pain" is more intense than an "ache".

a dull ache	*ein dumpfer Schmerz*
a slight pain	*ein schwacher Schmerz*
a stabbing pain	*ein stechender Schmerz*
an excruciating pain	*ein fürchterlicher Schmerz*
to be in pain	*Schmerzen haben*
aches and pains	*Wehwehchen*

"Aches and pains" is a fixed expression – the word order cannot be changed!

to ease (the) pain	*die Schmerzen lindern*
= to alleviate [əˈliːvɪeɪt] / relieve (the) pain	

to take it easy *(idiom)*	*locker angehen*
a splitting headache	*teuflische Kopfschmerzen*
a slight headache	*leichte Kopfschmerzen*
an upset stomach	*ein verdorbener Magen*
the thing is,	*die Sache ist die,*
Get well soon!	*Gute Besserung!*
to sustain an injury *(formal)*	*eine Verletzung erleiden*
= **to be injured** / to suffer an injury	
a slight / serious injury	*eine leichte / schwere Verletzung*
to be / hang in the balance *(idiom)*	*in der Schwebe sein*
to be in a critical condition	*in einem lebensbedrohlichen Zustand sein*
cuts and bruises	*leichte Verletzungen*

"Cuts and bruises" is a fixed expression – the word order cannot be changed!

"**Ms**" [məz] or [mɪz] is used as the formal title in front of a woman's name whether she is married or not. p. 196

to have a temperature	*Fieber haben*	p. 124
fatal [ˈfeɪtl] ❗	*tödlich*	p. 122
ambulance ❗	*Krankenwagen*	p. 132
to die <u>from</u> an injury / a wound [wuːnd]	*an einer Wunde / Verletzung sterben*	
to die <u>of</u> an illness	*an einer Krankheit sterben*	

1. Complete the following sentences using the correct preposition.

1. She died _____ cancer last year.

2. Why did she blame me _____ his mistake?

3. Are you allergic _____ pollen? –

   Yes, that's why I suffer _____ hayfever.

4. Many soldiers died _____ their injuries.

5. It was love _____ first sight.

6. In Britain, young people are allowed to get married

   _____ the age of 16.

7. Do you believe _____ ghosts?

2. All of the following words have something to do with families. Translate the German words to complete the diagram.

Die Familie Brown   *in der Familie liegen*   *Familienbande*
Großfamilie   *engste Familie*   *liebevolle Familie*
gestörte Familie

3. Choose the correct phrasal verb to complete each of these sentences. Make sure the new sentence is grammatically correct.

> to clear up – to come forward – to come over –
> to get over – to go round – to pull through – to run into

1. What time can you _____ tonight?

2. The police have asked anyone who might have seen the attacker

   to _____. Apparently, his victim

   is going to _____.

3. I _____ my old maths teacher at

   the match last week.

4. There's a nasty stomach bug _____

   at the moment. –

   I know, I had it over the weekend and I'm only just

   _____ it.

5. Your cold should _____ soon.

4. Combine each word on the left with one on the right to find expressions to do with relationships. Then translate them into German.

blind	bachelor	_____
single	marriage	_____
failed	person	_____
confirmed	date	_____

5. **Underline the idiom in each sentence. Then replace it with a similar expression from the box.**

> to relax and enjoy o.s. – to be very kind and generous –
> to relax and rest – to feel unwell – to not stop talking –
> to have serious doubts about s.th. –
> to have had enough of s.th. – to be extremely happy –
> to get on extremely well with s.o. – to get married

1. He talks nineteen to the dozen. _____

2. Your presentation went extremely well. You can go out and let your hair down tonight. _____

3. I met her at a party last week and we immediately got on like a house on fire. _____

4. I've just been out for a run and now I need to take it easy!

_____

5. Although she might seem very cold, she really has a heart of gold. _____

6. I'm beginning to have second thoughts about going to the conference next week. _____

7. They've finally decided to tie the knot. _____

8. I'm sick and tired of her complaining all the time.

_____

9. James has been feeling under the weather for a few days – I think he should see a doctor. _____

10. She's been walking on air all day. _____

6. **Combine these verbs with the nouns below to complete the expressions. Then translate them into German.**

to run	to bite	to grind	to clench	to pick
to furrow	to drum			

1. _____ one's nails   _____

2. _____ one's fingers   _____
   through one's hair

3. _____ one's fingers   _____
   on the table

4. _____ one's teeth   _____

5. _____ one's nose   _____

6. _____ one's fist   _____

7. _____ one's brow   _____

7. **Complete the following sentences using the correct verb.**

1. It only takes one bite from an infected mosquito to

   _____ malaria.

2. Little children _____ a lot of bugs when
   they start having more contact with other children.

3. People who smoke are more likely to _____
   lung cancer than those who do not.

4. He _____ multiple injuries in the crash.

5. This injection will help to _____ the pain.

6. Can you _____ a cold if you go outside with
   wet hair?

Famous political figures

Who are these famous British and American political figures?

1. He entered Parliament in 1900 as a **Conservative MP**, then joined the Liberals in 1904 and became **Home Secretary** in 1910. Over the next two decades he **held** many high **posts** in both Liberal and Conservative governments. The king asked him to **form a government** in 1940. His leadership and speeches **were a source of inspiration to** the British during the war. Many people consider him to be the greatest British prime minister of the 20th century.

2. He was **sworn into office** on a plane following the assassination of President Kennedy. The next year he **delivered a famous speech** in which he talked about a "Great Society". He **proposed** sweeping anti-poverty and civil rights legislation, **signing the Civil Rights Act** of 1964 and the Voting Rights Act in 1965. However, he also involved the US in the unpopular Vietnam War. It was because of anti-war protests that he **dropped his bid for** re-election in 1968.

3. This British politician was **elected to Parliament** in 1959, **rose up through the ranks** of the Conservative party, became **Secretary of State for Education** in 1970 and then **won three general elections in a row**. This person was famous for **laying down the law**, reducing the power of trade unions and privatizing nationalized industries. Controversial **policies** such as the introduction of the poll tax and opposition to any closer integration with Europe led to a leadership challenge, **prompting her to resign as** party leader in 1990. She was Britain's first female prime minister.

4. This **Democratic president took office** in 1993 for the first of two terms. A year later, he was not able to push through a bill providing health care for all Americans. However, during his administration, the US enjoyed more peace and economic well-being than at any past time. **On the world stage** he worked hard to try to **bring peace to** the **Middle East** and to Northern Ireland. As a result of **issues** surrounding his relationship with a White House intern, he became the second US **president to be impeached** by the House of Representatives. He was tried and **found not guilty** by the Senate.

Answers: p. 200

Talking about politics

The word **"politics"** refers to the world of politics or the subject. It is usually followed by a singular verb without any article, e.g. "He thinks politics is boring.", "I'm studying politics at university.".

"Politics" can also refer to political beliefs. If this is the case, a plural verb is used, e.g. "What are her politics?" *(politische Einstellung)*.

to enter (*also:* go into) politics — *in die Politik gehen*

The word **"policy"** is used to talk about plans or ideas, especially in politics, business or economics, e.g. "What's the government's policy on crime?" *(Politik)*.

to hold a (government) post	*einen Regierungsposten innehaben*
to form a government	*eine Regierung bilden*
to be sworn into office	*vereidigt werden*
to deliver a speech *(formal)*	*eine Rede halten*
to propose legislation	*ein Gesetz vorschlagen*
to sign an Act	*ein Gesetz unterzeichnen*
to rise up through the ranks	*sich hocharbeiten*
to win a general election	*Parlamentswahlen gewinnen*
in a row [rəʊ] *(idiom)* = in succession	*hintereinander*
to lay down the law (to s.o.) *(idiom)*	*(jdm.) Vorschriften machen*
to prompt s.o. to do s.th.	*jdn. dazu bringen, etw. zu tun*
to take office	*das Amt antreten*
on the world stage	*auf der Weltbühne*
to bring peace	*Frieden stiften*
to impeach the president	*den Präsidenten wegen Amtsvergehen anklagen*
to find s.o. not guilty (of a crime)	*jdn. für unschuldig befinden*

The name of a political party always begins with a capital letter in English, otherwise the meaning changes:
"a Conservative MP", i.e. a member of the Conservative party
"a conservative MP", i.e. an MP who does not like change
"the Democratic president", i.e. the president is a Democrat
"the democratic president", i.e. the president supports democracy

In Britain, the head of government departments is often called the **"Secretary of State for (Education** / Trade)". Exceptions include the **"Home Secretary"** (*Innenminister/in*), the "Foreign Secretary" (*Außenminister/in*), the "Chancellor of the Exchequer" (*Finanzminister/in*), who is head of the Treasury. In the US, the "Secretary of State" is the head of the State Department, which is in charge of foreign affairs.

to be a source of inspiration <u>to</u> s.o.	*eine Inspirationsquelle für jdn. sein*
to drop a bid <u>for</u> s.th.	*sich von / aus etw. zurückziehen*
to elect s.o. <u>to</u> Parliament	*jdn. in das Parlament wählen*
<u>Middle</u> East	*Naher Osten*
issue [ˈɪʃuː]	*Thema* p. 55

The many faces of immigration

Over the past fifty years, we have seen more people **seeking refuge from** war, persecution or disaster than ever before. In recent years, there have been **heated debates** in Europe over immigration and **asylum seekers**. But much of the time, people are getting confused by the terminology, so let us begin by briefly examining who **is on the move** and why.

Some people are **economic migrants** who **make a conscious decision to** leave their country. They do so **in the hope of** finding a better life. These people are able to return home **at will** and it is also **safe for** them to return.

So-called "environmental refugees" **are forced to** flee because of floods, famine or other **natural disasters**. Whilst they are similar to "refugees" because of their forced flight, their government is **sympathetic towards** them and they still have rights.

Refugees, on the other hand, have to flee to save their lives or preserve their freedom and **seek sanctuary** in a second country. The 1951 Convention Relating to the Status of Refugees states that a person is a refugee if they have left their home country and are unable or unwilling to return to it because they **fear** persecution on account of their "race, religion, nationality, **membership of** a particular social group, or political opinion".

Some refugees might be "**illegal immigrants**". Governments often refuse to **issue a passport to** known political dissidents. So refugees may not be able to **obtain the necessary documents** to leave their own country and enter another **by legal means**. As governments are **strengthening border controls** in order to **stop the flow of illegal immigrants**, it is more likely that **the latter** will use false documents or turn to human smugglers.

"Asylum seekers" are those who have formally **applied for asylum**, and are **awaiting a decision on** this. If their application is accepted, they are officially classed refugees. Sadly, it is this group of people that is being **discriminated against** and **treated with mistrust** and even hatred by some members of the **general public**.

Talking about immigration

asylum [əˈsaɪləm] **seeker**	*Asylsuchende/r*
economic migrant	*Wirtschaftsflüchtling*
illegal immigrant	*illegale/r Einwanderin/Einwanderer*
to immigrate <u>to</u> a country	*in ein Land einwandern*
to apply <u>for</u> asylum	*sich um Asyl bewerben*

to seek refuge from s.th. *Zuflucht vor etw. suchen*

Remember, "to seek" is an irregular verb (sought, sought). This expression can also be used figuratively, e.g. "She sought / found refuge in religion.".

heated debate over / about s.th.	*hitzige Debatte über etw.*
to be on the move *(idiom)*	*unterwegs sein*
to make a conscious decision to do s.th.	*eine bewusste Entscheidung treffen, etw. zu tun*
at will	*beliebig*
to be safe for s.o. to do s.th.	*ungefährlich sein, etw. zu tun*
to be forced to do s.th.	*gezwungen sein, etw. zu machen*
to seek sanctuary	*Zuflucht suchen*
to issue [ˈɪʃuː] **a passport to s.o.**	*jdm. einen Pass ausstellen*

The verb "to issue" is usually used in an official context.

to obtain a document *ein Dokument erhalten*

"To obtain" is a more formal way of saying "to get".

to strengthen border controls	*Grenzkontrollen verstärken*
to stop the flow of illegal immigrants	*das Eindringen von illegalen Einwanderern stoppen*

in the hope of <u>doing</u> s.th.	*in der Hoffnung, etw. zu tun*
natural <u>disaster</u>	*Naturkatastrophe*
to be sympathetic <u>towards</u> s.o.	*mit jdm. sympathisieren*
sympathetic **!**	*verständnisvoll*
to fear s.th.	*Angst vor etw. haben*

There is no preposition – it is a little more formal than "to be afraid <u>of</u> s.th.".

membership <u>of</u> s.th.	*Mitgliedschaft in etw.*
<u>by</u> **legal means**	*mit legalen Mitteln*
<u>the</u> **latter** *(formal)*	*letzteres*

If "latter" is used as a pronoun, it is preceded by the article "the". It can also be used as an adjective before a noun to refer to the end of something as opposed to the beginning, e.g. "the latter half of 1999".

to await a decision <u>on</u> s.th. *eine Entscheidung über etw. erwarten*

"To await s.th." is a more formal way of saying "to wait for s.th.". And note that "await" is not followed by a preposition.

to discriminate <u>against</u> s.o.	*jdn. diskriminieren*
to <u>treat</u> s.o. with mistrust	*jdm. mit Misstrauen begegnen*
the (general) public !	*die Öffentlichkeit*

p. 131

Call for witnesses

Police are appealing for witnesses to a near **fatal** stabbing in York over the weekend. The 24-year-old victim was viciously attacked at 1.23 a.m. on Saturday morning when he left a nightclub. Two men were **arrested on suspicion of** attempted **murder** following the incident and have since been released. PC Tim Wilson said "We are **making every effort** to find those responsible. I would urge anyone who might have seen anything to **come forward** to help us with our enquiries."

The jury deliberates

The jury is to **return its verdict** *in the Chance case today. The defendant Jason Hicks has been* **charged with** *first-degree murder. If guilty, he could* **face the death penalty**. *However, his* **lawyers** *are concerned that he will not have a fair trial due to the extensive media coverage …*

Juror 1: Hicks might be a **petty criminal** and have **done a bit of time**, but up to now he's not been **mixed up** in anything violent. It just doesn't **ring true**.

Juror 2: As far as I'm concerned, it's an **open-and-shut case** – Hicks was caught more or less **red-handed**. If you ask me, he should **be put away** for life.

Juror 6: **Hang on a minute**! We don't actually know whether Hicks *was* at the **scene of the crime** when Chance was killed. He claims he was **passing by** when he saw someone running out of the door and that's why he went in.

Juror 12: Ok, calm down everyone! I think we should go back and **review the evidence** before we **jump to any conclusions**. And let's not forget, everyone is **innocent until proven guilty**!

Find the expression on the right which means the same as each of the phrasal verbs.

1. to come forward	a) to go past
2. *to be mixed up in s.th.	b) to offer help or information
3. to pass by	c) to be involved in s.th.

Talking about crime and criminals

petty criminal	*Kleinkriminelle/r*
convicted criminal	*verurteilte/r Verbrecher/in*
hardened criminal	*Gewohnheitsverbrecher/in*
common criminal	*gewöhnliche/r Kriminelle/r*
petty crime	*Bagatelldelikt*
heinous ['hi:nəs] crime	*abscheuliches Verbrechen*
serious crime	*schweres Verbrechen*
to tackle crime	*Verbrechen bekämpfen*
to commit a crime	*ein Verbrechen begehen*

Talking about prison

to do time *(inf., idiom)*	*im Gefängnis sitzen*
to serve a (prison) sentence	*eine Strafe absitzen*
to put s.o. away *(inf.)*	
to put s.o. behind bars *(inf., idiom)*	*jdn. einsperren*
to send s.o. to prison	
to sentence s.o. to life (imprisonment)	*jdn. zu lebenslänglicher Haft verurteilen*

Talking about lawyers

The word "**lawyer**" describes a person who is qualified to advise people about the law and represent them in court. There are lawyers for the prosecution and lawyers for the defence (*AE* defense). In the US, lawyers are called "attorneys". In the UK, there are "barristers" (allowed to represent people in the higher courts) and "solicitors" (allowed to help people with legal matters, represent them in some courts and advise barristers).

to make every effort to do s.th.	*sich alle Mühe geben, etw. zu tun*	
to return a verdict	*ein Urteil fällen*	
to return a verdict of not guilty	*nicht schuldig sprechen*	
to face the death penalty	*die Todesstrafe erwarten*	
to ring true *(idiom)*	*glaubhaft klingen*	
open-and-shut case	*eindeutiger Fall*	
to catch s.o. red-handed *(idiom)*	*jdn. auf frischer Tat ertappen*	
Hang on a minute! *(inf.)*	*Warte mal!*	p. 180
the scene of the crime	*Tatort*	
You can also say "the crime scene".		
to review the evidence	*hier: die Beweislage (erneut) sichten*	
to jump to conclusions *(idiom)*	*voreilige Schlüsse ziehen*	
innocent until proven guilty	*im Zweifel für den Angeklagten*	
fatal ['feɪtl] **!**	*tödlich*	p. 122
to arrest s.o. <u>on</u> suspicion of s.th.	*jdn. wegen des Verdachts auf etw. verhaften*	
murder !	*Mord*	p. 131
to be charged <u>with</u> a crime	*wegen eines Verbrechens angeklagt sein*	

Wanted: dead or alive

Jesse James (1847–1882) and his brother Frank (1843–1915) were two of the most notorious outlaws of the American West.

When the Civil War **broke out**, the young brothers joined Quantrill's Confederate raiders, a band of guerrilla fighters. Jesse also rode with "Bloody" Bill Anderson's gang. After the end of the war, Jesse and Frank formed a gang and turned to a life of crime. Within a year, they **pulled off** a daring bank robbery, **making off with** $60,000 from the bank in Liberty, Missouri. Their crime spree continued for many years during which time they robbed banks in different states and also held up trains. However, this meant that they were always on the run. In a failed robbery attempt in 1876 most of the gang members were killed or captured – the James brothers had a narrow escape and managed to **get away**. It was after this that Jesse decided to lie low for a time. However, in 1879 he was up to his old tricks with a new gang, although this time it was short-lived. In 1881, Missouri governor Thomas T. Crittenden offered a $10,000 reward for their capture, dead or alive. On April 3, 1882, Jesse was shot in the back in St. Joseph, Missouri by Robert Ford, a gang member, for the reward. At the time of his death, Jesse James had been at large for sixteen years. To some he was a folk hero, to others simply a cold-blooded killer.

A few months after his brother's death, Frank decided to face the music and **turned himself in**. He was tried for murder and robbery in different states but was found not guilty.

Which expression means the same as each of the phrasal verbs?	
1. to break out	*a) to succeed in doing s.th. difficult*
2. to pull s.th. off	*b) to steal s.th.*
3. to make off with s.th.	*c) to allow o.s. to be arrested*
4. to get away	*d) to start suddenly*
5. to turn o.s. in	*e) to escape*

Talking about robbery

to rob	The verb "to rob" is used with a person or an institution, e.g. "She robbed the man.", "They robbed the bank.".
to steal	The verb "to steal" is used if you want to say you take something, e.g. "The thieves stole the painting.".
to burgle to burglarize *(AE)*	The verb "to burgle" is used for houses, e.g. "Her house was burgled last night.".
to break into *(inf.)* *also:* to break and enter	The verb "to break into" is used for buildings, vehicles and property, e.g. "Two thieves broke into his apartment.".
bank robbery bank heist ['haɪst]*(AE)*	*Bankraub*
to commit a robbery to do a heist *(AE)*	*einen Raubüberfall verüben*
to hold up (a bank, a train)	*(eine Bank, einen Zug) überfallen*
to turn to a life of crime to lead a life of crime	*eine Verbrecherlaufbahn einschlagen* *ein kriminelles Leben führen*
crime spree	*Verbrechenstour*

You can also go on a "shopping spree" *(Einkaufstour)* or a "spending spree" *(Kaufrausch).*

to be on the run *(idiom)*	*auf der Flucht sein*
to have a narrow escape *(idiom)*	*knapp entkommen*
to be up to one's old tricks *(idiom)*	*in die alten Gewohnheiten verfallen*
to be up to s.th. *(inf., idiom)*	*etw. im Schilde führen / etw. vorhaben*

If someone is "up to something", he or she is usually doing something forbidden, in secret.

If someone asks you "What's up?", it is an informal way of asking "What's wrong?".

to offer a reward	*eine Belohnung aussetzen*
to be at large	*auf freiem Fuß sein*
to face the music *(idiom)*	*für etw. geradestehen*
to find s.o. not guilty (of a crime)	*jdn. (eines Verbrechens) für nicht schuldig befinden*
to lie low *(idiom)*	*untertauchen*

If a person "lies low", then he or she is hiding from something and trying not to attract attention.
However, if an illness "lays someone low" *(idiom)*, it makes the person weak and unable to do things that he or she would normally do.

to try s.o. for (a crime)	*jdn. (wegen eines Verbrechens) vor Gericht stellen*

Our ageing population

Welcome to today's programme on our ageing population. Professor Helen Carter, an eminent sociologist, has joined me in the studio today. Professor Carter, what kind of problems are we up against?
Ageing populations are a worldwide phenomenon. The main reason for this is a decline in fertility rates and greater life expectancy. In addition, the so-called baby boomer generation is starting to retire and this is accelerating the trend. The economic implications of this are enormous: the ratio of pensioners to the number of people of working age is increasing rapidly. We need to take this challenge and turn it into an opportunity!

What can we do?
Well, first of all, we have to stop seeing the elderly as being a drain on our resources. Older people are not a burden on society – they have a key role to play, both socially and economically. We need to start thinking about how we can work together so that we can profit from their experience and so that they can continue to make a contribution.

Can you give some examples?
One of the most obvious ways is to try to keep older people in active employment for a longer period. But this means that many employers will have to change their ageist attitudes.
Older people are active consumers with important spending power which will contribute to the economy. Because they have time on their hands, many of them also regularly do some kind of voluntary work and often provide essential childcare for their families, enabling parents to go out to work. And don't underestimate the political clout of the "silver generation" – senior citizens are more likely to vote and many are actively involved in pressure groups.

But, of course, we have responsibilities, too, don't we?
Absolutely – it's not a one-way street! The break-up of traditional family structures means that elderly people can become isolated and have to fend for themselves. We must remove the barriers between the generations to create good social support networks and at the same time, we have to make sure that services are in place to enable people to live life to the full as they grow older.

Talking about ageing

Be careful with the spelling of "**ageing**" – in British English there is an "e",
in American English there is not.

baby boomer generation *(idiom)*	*geburtenstarke Jahrgänge (der Nachkriegszeit)*

Older people are also referred to as the "**elderly**", "seniors" *(AE)*, the "**silver generation**" or "grey generation" (the last two on account of their hair colour). These are just some of the euphemisms used to talk about old people.

p. 164

pensioner	*Rentner/in*
senior citizen	*ältere/r Bürger/in*
to be up against a problem	*mit einem Problem zu tun haben*

Remember you "have a problem <u>doing</u> something".

fertility rate	*Fruchtbarkeitsrate*
greater life expectancy	*höhere Lebenserwartung*
economic implications of s.th. (<u>for</u> s.th.)	*wirtschaftliche Auswirkungen von etw. (auf etw.)*

The word "implication" is usually used in the plural when referring to possible effects or results.

the ratio of s.th. to s.th.	*das Verhältnis von etw. zu etw.*
to turn s.th. into an opportunity	*etw. in eine Gelegenheit verwandeln*
to be a drain on s.o.'s resources	*jdm. auf der Tasche liegen*
to have a key role to play	*eine Schlüsselrolle spielen*
to make a contribution (to s.th.)	*einen Beitrag (zu etw.) leisten*
to change one's attitude (towards / to s.th.)	*seine Einstellung (gegenüber / zu etw.) ändern*
to have time on one's hands *(idiom)*	*Zeit zur Verfügung haben*
to do voluntary work = to volunteer	*ehrenamtlich tätig sein*
political clout *(inf.)*	*politischer Einfluss*

If you have "clout", you have the authority to make decisions. It is often used in combination with the adjectives "political", "economic" and "financial". "To clout s.o." is an informal expression and means "to hit s.o.".

pressure group	*Interessenverband*
lobby *(AE)*	
It's not a one-way street!	*Es ist keine Einbahnstraße!*
to fend for o.s.	*sich alleine durchschlagen*
to be in place *(idiom)*	*da sein*
to live life to the full *(idiom)*	*das Leben voll ausleben*
to be a burden <u>on</u> society	*der Gesellschaft zur Last fallen*
<u>spending</u> **power**	*Kaufkraft*
to be actively involved <u>in</u> s.th.	*sich sehr für etw. engagieren*

Lifelong learning

Presenter: Good evening and welcome to the last programme in this series on lifelong learning. Today we are looking at the U3A movement in Britain and I have three of its members here in the studio with me. First of all, what does "U3A" actually mean?

Guest 1: U3A **stands for** the University of the Third Age. It's an organization of like-minded older people no longer in full-time employment who have joined together to share and expand their knowledge. The word "University" is used in its original sense of people coming together to share and pursue learning in all its forms. There are groups all around the country, which are run entirely by volunteers.

Presenter: How does it work? What curriculum do you follow?

Guest 2: There's no curriculum – the courses on offer are defined by the know-how and skills of the members in each group. And because our members come from all walks of life – some of them used to be academics, businessmen or work in the caring professions – there's a wealth of knowledge **on** which to **draw**. Many of our members know their subjects inside out.

Guest 3: It's really quite simple. If someone is particularly knowledgeable about a subject, let's say painting, they might decide to run a course or study group on it. And as soon as a few other people have **signed up**, they can get started. Groups are run on a regular basis, often in people's own homes.

Presenter: Do people need qualifications to join?

Guest 1: None whatsoever! And people also don't get marks, do exams or get qualifications. The U3A is all about the enjoyment of learning – it is not a means to an end but the means *is* the end.

Which expression on the right means the same as each of these phrasal verbs?

1. to stand for s.th.	a) to make use of s.th. to help you do s.th.
2. to draw on s.th.	b) to register (for s.th.)
3. to sign up (for s.th.)	c) to be short for s.th.

Talking about knowledge

"Knowledge" is uncountable. However, unlike other uncountable nouns it can sometimes be used with an indefinite article with a qualifying adjective, e.g. "He has a detailed knowledge of Greek." *(Kenntnisse)*.

to expand one's knowledge	*sein Wissen erweitern*
to have a thorough knowledge <u>of</u> s.th.	*ein fundiertes Wissen über etw. besitzen*
a wealth of knowledge	*Wissensschatz*
to know s.th. inside out *(idiom)*	*etw. bis ins kleinste Detail kennen*
to be knowledgeable <u>about</u> s.th.	*sehr bewandert in etw. sein*

Talking about education

Here are some common expressions – in the second column you will find a few alternative suggestions to help you to improve your written English:

to do an exam	to sit an exam	*eine Prüfung ablegen*
to get a qualification	to obtain a qualification	*eine Qualifikation erwerben*
to go to a lecture	to attend a lecture	*eine Vorlesung besuchen*
to do a subject	to study a subject	*etw. studieren*

like-minded people	*Gleichgesinnte*
to be in full-time employment	*vollzeitbeschäftigt sein*
to pursue learning	*Bildung nachgehen*
to follow a curriculum	*einem Lehrplan folgen*
to come from all walks of life *(idiom)*	*aus allen Gesellschaftsschichten kommen*
caring professions	*Sozialberufe*
to run a course	*einen Kurs anbieten*
on a regular basis	*regelmäßig*
to be all about s.th.	*um etw. gehen*
a means to an end *(idiom)*	*ein Mittel zum Zweck*
to be <u>on</u> offer	*im Angebot sein*

"**Used to**" *(früher)* is used to express past habits and repeated actions in the past. It is followed by the infinitive. When asking a question, you use "did", e.g. "Did you use to work here?" (note the spelling – the "d" of "used" is dropped after "did"). When forming the negative, you say "used not to" (it is better style than using "did"), e.g. "It used not to be like that.".

The German word *"Wissenschaftler/in"* is often mistranslated. An **"academic"** teaches or does research at university. A "scholar" is a person who knows a great deal about a subject, particularly a non-scientific one. Only use "scientist" if you mean a natural scientist *(Naturwissenschaftler/in)*. p. 118

to get a mark *(BE)*	*eine Note bekommen*

Remember, in Britain you are given a "mark" in tests (in the US it is called a "grade"). However, for formal qualifications (such as GCSEs, A levels, etc.) you are awarded a "grade", e.g. "He obtained three A grades at A level.".

Conference on Creating Sustainable Cities

General information

Almost half of the global population now lives in cities, and this proportion is set to grow. Yet our cities have a negative impact on the environment and fail to provide acceptable living conditions for hundreds of millions of people. A large number live in overcrowded slums, lacking adequate shelter and do not have easy access to clean water, sanitation or electricity.

With more and more people being drawn to urban centres, decision-makers are now faced with the task of how to resolve urban problems and how to put quality of life back at the top of the agenda.

Some of the issues we will be addressing:

- "A clean, green, safe environment": creating urban centres that are in tune with our environment.

- "Crime-ridden cities – a thing of the past": tackling urban crime and creating a sense of community.

- "Green travel": creating efficient and green transportation systems to reduce the volume of traffic on the roads and ease congestion.

- "Reducing the pressures of city life": adopting imaginative approaches to the use of green space.

- "Safeguarding the countryside": establishing a green belt around new and existing cities to check the unrestricted sprawl of large built-up areas and to protect rural areas.

- "Reflecting people's basic needs": providing the appropriate technology and infrastructure to support the changing needs of inhabitants.

In English, the word "city" only refers to a large and important town or the political, legal and administrative institutions of a city, e.g. "the city hospital".

If you are referring to the centre of a city or town, you talk about the "centre" or "city centre". In the US, people talk about "downtown".

When people talk about "The City" in Britain, they are referring to "the City of London" which is the area in central London in which many financial institutions are located.

Talking about streets and roads

A "street" is a road in a town or city with houses or buildings on either side of it. It tends to refer more to the life around it. A "road" can be in a town or in the country. "Road" refers more to the traffic on it or the actual surface." Look at these examples:
"This street is dangerous – you shouldn't walk here on your own at night."
"This road is dangerous – accidents regularly happen here."

Some expressions are only used with one or other of the words, e.g.
"street light" *(Straßenlaterne)*, "street corner" *(Straßenecke)*,
"high street" *(Hauptstraße)*
"road accident" *(Verkehrsunfall)*, "road safety" *(Verkehrssicherheit)*,
"roadworks" *(Straßenbauarbeiten)* (always plural in *BE*, never plural in *AE*),
"road map / atlas" *(Straßenkarte)*

on the roads	*auf den Straßen*
to have a negative impact ['ɪmpækt] **on s.th.**	*eine negative Auswirkung auf etw. haben*
to fail to do s.th.	*hier: nicht in der Lage sein, etw. zu tun*
to have (easy) access to s.th.	*(leichten) Zugang zu etw. haben*

"**Urban**" ['ɜːbn] is the adjective which means relating to towns or cities. It is usually only used before a noun, e.g. "urban area" *(städtisch, Stadt-)*. The opposite of "urban" is "**rural**" ['rʊərəl] *(ländlich)*.

to be faced with s.th.	*mit etw. konfrontiert sein*	
quality of life	*Lebensqualität*	
to put s.th. at the top of the agenda *(idiom)*	*etw. ganz oben auf die Tagesordnung setzen*	
to address an issue ['ɪʃuː]	*hier: sich mit etw. befassen*	p. 55
to be in tune with s.th. *(idiom)*	*mit etw. in Einklang sein*	
to be a thing of the past *(idiom)*	*der Vergangenheit angehören*	
to tackle a problem	*ein Problem angehen*	
volume of traffic	*Verkehrsdichte*	
to ease congestion	*Verkehrsüberlastung verringern*	
to adopt an imaginative approach to s.th.	*kreativ an eine Sache herangehen*	

The qualifying adjective can be changed in this expression. Other ones which are often used with it are "cautious", "pragmatic" or "aggressive".

to safeguard the countryside	*die Landschaft schützen*

"Countryside" refers to the land and scenery of a rural area. "The country" (no plural) refers to rural areas not towns, e.g. "I live in the country.".

built-up area	*bebautes Gebiet*

Remember, "**environment**" not only refers to the natural world *(Umwelt)* but also to our surroundings *(Umgebung)* and social surroundings *(Umfeld)*.

adequate ❗	*ausreichend*
appropriate ❗	*adäquat*

Interfaith week

"Everyone has the right to **freedom of thought**, conscience and religion; this right includes **freedom to change** his religion or belief, and freedom, either alone or in community with others and **in public** or **private**, to manifest his religion or belief in teaching, **practice**, worship and observance."

Article 18, Universal Declaration of Human Rights

This week the University and the Student Union are **celebrating faith** and diversity **on campus**. We have a multi-faith community in which students may freely **practise their religion** and which is **sensitive to** all beliefs.

The aim of this week is not to convert anyone. It **is about** promoting dialogue between different religious groups and increasing understanding. We wish to encourage people to **be more tolerant of** other faiths and cultures so as to **break down barriers** within the community.

Presentations, forums, social events and visits to local **places of worship** encourage students to **raise questions** and have conversations about different **approaches to** faith and spirituality.

Last year's week **was a resounding success** – here are some of the reactions:

"I was very honoured to be able to **participate in** Interfaith Week and share my beliefs with others. I believe it is very important to **set an example to** others so that all the different faiths in our community can exist peacefully **side by side**."

"I'm a **practising Christian** and thought it was a fantastic experience – with a lot of focus on our **common ground** and values."

"Although I don't **believe in** anything – I'm an atheist – I was impressed by the fact that everyone was very open-minded and didn't try to **put me under pressure to** join their particular group."

Talking about belief

to celebrate faith	*den Glauben feiern*

In this case, "faith" is uncountable as it means a belief in God or gods, e.g. "Faith in God has helped her through difficult times.". However, if "faith" is used to mean a religion, it is countable, e.g. "There are representatives of different faiths here – including the Christian, Jewish and Muslim faiths.". In a non-religious sense, it means "confidence" or "trust" and is uncountable, e.g. "He had great faith in her ability.".

place of worship	*Gotteshaus, Ort der Verehrung*
to believe <u>in</u> s.th.	*an etw. glauben*
to hold a belief	*glauben*

freedom of thought	*Gedankenfreiheit*
to have the freedom to do s.th.	*die Freiheit haben, etw. zu tun*
to be about s.th.	*um etw. gehen*
to break down barriers	*Barrieren einreißen*
to raise a question	*eine Frage aufwerfen*
an approach to s.th.	*eine Herangehensweise an etw.*
to be a resounding success	*ein durchschlagender Erfolg sein*
to set an example to s.o.	*jdm. etw. vorleben*
common ground *(idiom)*	*Gemeinsamkeit*
to put s.o. under pressure to do s.th.	*jdn. unter Druck setzen, etw. zu tun*

<u>in</u> public	*öffentlich, in der Öffentlichkeit*
<u>in</u> private	*privat*

Remember, in Britain the verb is "to practi<u>s</u>e" and the noun is "**practice**". Other words which follow this rule include "to advise" *(beraten)* and "advice" *(Ratschlag)*, "to license" *(zulassen)* and "licence" *(Lizenz)*. In American English the noun and the verb are both spelt with a "c".   p. 116

And remember, you practise <u>doing</u> something, e.g. "He practised walking on his hands.".

to practise a religion	*eine Religion ausüben*
a practi<u>s</u>ing Christian !	*ein praktizierender Christ* *eine praktizierende Christin*

Note the word "Christ" refers to "Jesus Christ" in English. A "Christian" *(Christ)* is someone whose religion is Christianity. The adjective is "Christian" *(christlich)*. The German word *Konfession* is translated as "denomination".

on campus	*auf dem Campus*

Note there is no article in English.

to be <u>sensitive to</u> s.th. !	*sensibel für etw. sein*

p. 132

to be tolerant <u>of</u> / towards s.th.	*gegenüber etw. tolerant sein*
to participate <u>in</u> s.th.	*an etw. teilnehmen*
side <u>by</u> side	*Seite an Seite*

1. Complete the following sentences using the correct preposition.

1. Princess Diana was a source of inspiration _____ many people.

2. He was very sensitive _____ criticism because he was afraid _____ making mistakes.

3. New legislation has been brought in to stop discrimination _____ minorities.

4. She was arrested _____ suspicion _____ espionage but was later charged _____ treason.

5. These DVDs are _____ special offer this week.

6. He's actively involved _____ charity work.

7. It is very important to be tolerant _____ other religions.

2. Which word fits in each case? Cross out the incorrect word in each of these sentences.

1. He studied economics because he was interested in going into (policy / politics) later on.

2. What's this company's (policy / politics) on working from home?

3. I always tried to avoid talking about (policy / politics) with her. Her (policy / politics) (are / is) her own affair.

4. Did you read about Britain's new foreign (policy / politics).

5. Many people decide to take out a life insurance (policy / politics) when they have children.

3. **Choose the correct expression to complete each of these sentences. Use the British English spelling and use the verbs in the right tense.**

1. The thieves _____ (break into / hold up) the museum because they wanted to _____ (rob / steal) the painting. Afterwards, they decided to _____ _____ (lay low / lie low) for a few weeks.

2. It is a basic human right to be allowed to _____ (practice / practise) a religion.

3. The government tried to reduce the volume of traffic on the _____ (roads / streets) in an attempt to improve _____ (road / street) safety.

4. We have to improve our attitude towards the elderly and not just talk about their responsibilities towards us – it's not a one-way _____ (road / street)!

5. This history book was written by a _____ (scholar / scientist).

6. You'll need good _____ (grades / marks) at A level if you want to study medicine.

7. Is Tom ill? – Yes, the flu _____ (lay low / lie low) since the beginning of the week.

8. (Scholars / Scientists) _____ have made exciting breakthroughs in stem cell research.

9. This latest decision was very _____ (democratic / Democratic) – everyone voted on it.

4. Find the phrasal verb which means the same as each expression below. Combine a verb from the left with the prepositions on the right. Then match each one to its meaning below.

to be mixed	for s.th.
to break	s.th. off
to make	off with s.th.
to pull	out
to sign	up for s.th.
to stand	up in s.th.

a) to manage to do s.th. difficult   _____

b) to be part of s.th.   _____

c) to steal s.th.   _____

d) to put one's name down for s.th.   _____

e) to begin abruptly   _____

f) to be an abbreviation for s.th.   _____

5. The words in the middle have been jumbled up. Find out the words – the German translation will help. Then combine one of the words on the left with the ones you have worked out to find expressions relating to immigration.

economic	_____	ekeres	*Suchender*
to apply for	_____	tginarm	*Migrant*
border	_____	cutranasy	*Zuflucht*
asylum	_____	ulmays	*Asyl*
to seek	_____	rangmitim	*Einwanderer*
illegal	_____	scoltron	*Kontrollen*

6. Choose the correct idiom to complete each of these sentences.

1. She _____ using her mobile in the exam.
   a) was caught red-handed   b) laid down the law

2. After a long trial, the drug dealer _____ for six years last week.
   a) did time   b) was put behind bars

3. He's worked as a lawyer in the US for years and knows the legal system _____.
   a) on the run   b) inside out

4. This new technology _____ the needs of the younger generation.
   a) is in tune with   b) is up to

5. Now that so much information is available online, will libraries soon _____?
   a) be a thing of the past   b) be facing the music

6. Even though they've retired, they don't seem to _____ _____.
   a) be up to their old tricks   b) have time on their hands

7. I'm afraid your arguments _____.
   a) are not in tune   b) don't ring true

8. My friends are all very different and _____.
   a) come from all walks of life b) rise up through the ranks

In the war zone

66 The troops in this unit were originally sent in to **restore order** after **fierce fighting** **broke out** in the capital between two rival factions. However, they are now **caught up in** a civil war and live in constant **fear of their lives**.

Many of the troops in this unit **joined the army** straight after school and **were not prepared for** the horrors awaiting them here. They have to **put up with** terrible conditions, which **are going from bad to worse**. They often eat and sleep **within firing range** of the local militia outpost and **are under constant pressure**, working 16-hour days **on average**. Whenever they go out on patrol they **are under threat** from bombs and snipers. Only yesterday, gunmen **shot at** a patrol, killing one of the soldiers. Later, one of the vehicles in the convoy was **blown up** by a car bomb.

As the **body count** rises, it is difficult to keep morale up. **Off the record**, many of them are now saying that the war is senseless. In fact there is no **end in sight** as both factions have **rejected a call for a ceasefire**. Thus, hopes for **establishing peace** in the region are fading fast.

Under the circumstances it is no surprise that many of them are now counting the days left till they can have a few days off, hoping they will **make it home in one piece**.

This is Dave Allen for *News at Ten*, reporting with the troops on the front line. 99

Which expression means the same as these phrasal verbs?	
1. to break out	*a) to have to accept s.th. bad or unpleasant*
2. to be caught up in s.th.	*b) to explode*
3. to put up with s.th.	*c) to be involved in s.th. unpleasant without wanting to be*
4. to blow up	*d) to start suddenly*

Talking about war

to wage war (against s.o. / s.th.) = to fight a war	*gegen jdn. / etw. Krieg führen*
to declare war (on s.o. / s.th.)	*jdm. / etw. den Krieg erklären*
to go to war	*in den Krieg ziehen*
to be at war (with s.o.)	*sich im Kriegszustand befinden*
to avert [əˈvɜːt] war	*den Krieg abwenden*

The first three expressions are also used in other contexts, especially when showing a determined effort to stop or control something, e.g.
"The war on terrorism."
"This is an important step in the war against drugs."
"The Prime Minister is waging war on underage drinking."
"Politicians have declared war on organized crime."

Talking about war – euphemisms

Euphemisms are neutral words or expressions that are used when talking about something which might be found unpleasant, embarrassing or upsetting. Military people (as well as politicians and newspapers) often use them to talk about war. Here are some examples: p. 164

body count	= number of people killed	*Anzahl der Todesopfer*
collateral damage	= civilian deaths	*Kollateralschaden*
friendly fire	= killing people on your own side	*Beschuss durch die eigenen Truppen*
to neutralize	= to kill	*töten*
soft target	= unprotected target	*weiches Ziel*

to restore order	*die Ordnung wiederherstellen*
fierce fighting	*erbitterter Kampf*
to be in fear of one's life	*Angst um sein Leben haben*
to join the army	*Soldat/in werden*
to go from bad to worse *(idiom)*	*vom Regen in die Traufe kommen*
within firing range	*in Schussweite*
off the record (≠ on the record) *(idiom)*	*inoffiziell*
no end in sight *(idiom)*	*kein Ende in Sicht*
to reject a call for a ceasefire	*eine Feuerpause ablehnen*
to establish peace	*den Frieden wiederherstellen*
under the circumstances	*unter diesen Umständen*
to make it home in one piece	*heil nach Hause kommen*

to be prepared <u>for</u> s.th.	*auf etw. vorbereitet sein*	
to <u>be</u> under pressure	*unter Druck stehen*	
<u>on</u> average	*im Durchschnitt*	p. 142
to be <u>under</u> threat of s.th.	*von etw. bedroht sein*	
to shoot <u>at</u> s.o. (*also:* to fire <u>on</u> s.o.)	*auf jdn. schießen*	

The Oklahoma City bombing

On 19 April 1995 just after 9 a.m., a massive bomb **went off** inside a rental truck, **blowing up** half of the Alfred P. Murrah Federal Building in Oklahoma City. 168 people were killed in the blast and over 500 others were injured. Until 11 September 2001, it was the deadliest act of terrorism in the U.S.

Only 90 minutes after the explosion, an Oklahoma Highway Patrol officer **pulled over** 27-year-old Timothy McVeigh for driving a car without a number plate. Hours before he was to be released, he was identified and charged with the bombing. The same day, Terry Nichols, an ex-army friend of McVeigh's, discovered that he was also wanted and voluntarily **gave himself up**.

McVeigh stood trial in 1997 and was found guilty of the bombing. The jury sentenced him to death and on 11 June 2001 he was executed by lethal injection. Nichols was tried separately and sentenced to life in prison. A third conspirator, Michael Fortier, was imprisoned for failing to warn the U.S. government of the attack.

McVeigh reportedly **carried out** the attack in retaliation for the bloody end to a siege near Waco, Texas.

Which expression means the same as each phrasal verb?	
1. to go off	*a) to stop s.o.*
2. to blow s.th. up	*b) to explode*
3. to pull s.o. over	*c) to allow o.s. to be arrested*
4. to give o.s. up	*d) to do s.th.*
5. to carry s.th. out	*e) to destroy s.th.*

> *If a vehicle or driver "pulls over", they go to the side of the road. If the police "pull someone over", they order the driver to stop.*

Hostages freed

Two female aid workers were finally set free last night after being held hostage for three weeks. During this time their fate had hung in the balance. Despite speculation that money might have changed hands, the government denied rumours that it had given in to blackmail and paid a ransom to secure their release. They received a warm welcome from their families, friends and members of the public when they landed this morning.

Talking about hostages

to hold s.o. hostage	*jdn. als Geisel halten*
to take s.o. hostage	*jdn. als Geisel nehmen*
to seize s.o. hostage	
to pay a ransom	*Lösegeld zahlen*
to demand a ransom	*Lösegeld fordern*
to hold s.o. to (*AE* for) ransom	*jdn. als Geisel festhalten*
to secure (a hostage's) release	*Freilassung einer Geisel sichern; hier: bewirken*
act of terrorism	*Terrorakt*
to be wanted	*(von der Polizei) gesucht werden*
to stand trial	*vor Gericht stehen*
to be on trial	
to find s.o. guilty (of a crime)	*jdn. für schuldig befinden*
to sentence s.o. to death	*jdn. zum Tode verurteilen*
to be executed by lethal injection	*hingerichtet werden durch eine tödliche Injektion*
to sentence s.o. to life in prison	*jdn. zu lebenslänglicher Haft verurteilen*
to set s.o. free (*also:* to free s.o.)	*jdn. freilassen*
to hang in the balance (*idiom*)	*in der Schwebe sein*
(*also:* to be in the balance)	
to change hands (*idiom*)	*den Besitzer wechseln*

If money "changes hands", it is given from one person to another in payment for something, often in a dishonest way.

to deny a rumour	*ein Gerücht dementieren*
to confirm a rumour	*ein Gerücht bestätigen*
to spread a rumour	*ein Gerücht verbreiten*
rumour mill	*Gerüchteküche*
to give in to blackmail	*sich erpressen lassen*
to give in to s.th.	*etw. nachgeben*
to receive a warm welcome	*herzlich empfangen werden*
to be killed <u>in</u> the blast	*bei der Explosion umkommen*
to be charged <u>with</u> (a crime)	*wegen eines Verbrechens angeklagt sein*
to warn s.o. <u>of</u> s.th.	*jdn. vor etw. warnen*
<u>in</u> retaliation for s.th.	*als Vergeltung für etw.*
public !	*Öffentlichkeit* p. 131

Global warming

Welcome to today's programme on climate change and global warming. Professor James Stevenson, an expert on climate change, has joined me in the studio today. Professor Stevenson, freak weather conditions, melting polar ice caps, natural disasters, shrinking habitats – every day we hear more alarming news. Where does responsibility lie?

In the past, the changes in our atmosphere were due to natural causes. Nowadays scientists believe that humans are largely to blame for them: we are burning fossil fuels and **heating up** the planet at the same time.

What impact is global warming having on our natural environment?

Climate change is disturbing the ecological balance with devastating consequences. Over the last 500 years, 844 species are known to have **died out**, and up to 16,000 others are now known to be threatened. But this may only be the tip of the iceberg – the real number facing extinction could be much higher. Conservationists argue that we have an ethical obligation to protect other species: we rely on ecosystems to provide food, oxygen and natural resources. In addition, the ice caps are melting and sea levels are rising. Because of this, some of the world's small island nations are now in danger of being obliterated.

What about the weather?

There have been dramatic changes in the weather. Severe droughts, fatal heat waves, lethal storms, hurricanes and flooding are on the rise and the effects are being felt across the globe.

*Have they also **been brought about** by global warming?*

The facts speak for themselves: the three warmest years on record have all occurred since 1998 and 19 of the warmest 20 since 1980.

So what now?

It's quite simple: our planet is at risk, we're all in the same boat and so we all need to take action.

Find the expression which means the same as each phrasal verb.

1. to heat s.th. up	*a) to become extinct*
2. to die out	*b) to cause s.th.*
3. to bring s.th. about	*c) to make s.th. warmer*

Talking about nature

The German word *"Natur"* can be translated in different ways in English.
"Nature" refers to the physical world including all living things, land and
sea. It does not have an article, e.g. "She's interested in nature so she's going
to work for a conservation organisation.".
The "countryside" refers to the land and scenery, e.g. "The Scottish
countryside is very wild and beautiful.".
The "**natural environment**" refers to all living and non-living things
that naturally occur on Earth, e.g. "We are destroying our natural
environment.".

natural disaster	*Naturkatastrophe*
freak of nature	*Laune der Natur*
climate change	*Klimawandel*
freak weather conditions	*außergewöhnliche Wetterbedingungen*
shrinking habitat	*schrumpfender Lebensraum*
alarming news	*beunruhigende Nachricht*
to have (*or* make) **an impact on s.th.**	*Auswirkungen auf etw. haben*

Note in English "impact" is in the singular!

to disturb the ecological balance	*das ökologische Gleichgewicht stören*
devastating consequences	*verheerende Auswirkungen*
the tip of the iceberg (*idiom*)	*die Spitze des Eisbergs*
to face extinction	*vom Aussterben bedroht sein*
to have an ethical obligation to do s.th.	*eine ethische Verpflichtung haben, etw. zu tun*
to be in danger of doing s.th.	*Gefahr laufen, etw. zu tun*
to be on the rise	*steigen*
to take action	*handeln, Maßnahmen ergreifen*

responsibility lies <u>with</u> ...	*die Verantwortung liegt bei ...*

Remember in English there is no article!

The German word *"früher"* is translated as "**in the past**" if the emphasis
is more on the time itself or the historical aspect, e.g. "What was life like
in the past?". *"Früher"* is translated as "used to" if the emphasis is on the
activity, e.g. "We used to have a cat.". It is only very rarely translated as "in
former times".

to blame s.o. for s.th. !	*jdm. die Schuld für etw. geben*	p. 130
fatal !	*tödlich*	

If something is "fatal", it causes death. If something is "**lethal**", it is very
dangerous and has the potential to cause death. p. 122

Remember, the noun is "**effect**" (*Auswirkung*) and the verb is "to <u>a</u>ffect"
(*beeinflussen*). The verb "to effect" means "to bring about, cause" (*bewirken*). p. 108

(to be) on record ['rekɔːd] (*idiom*)	*verzeichnet (sein)*
to be <u>at</u> risk	*in Gefahr sein*
to <u>be</u> in the same boat (*idiom*)	*im selben Boot sitzen*

Eighth Annual Conference on Ethics in the 21st Century

General information
The global challenges of the 21st century are increasingly complex, especially in the light of rapid advances in the fields of biotechnology and information technology. As some ethical boundaries are becoming blurred, people are finding it increasingly difficult to make the right moral choice. We – the public, researchers and governments – need to address the serious ethical issues raised by these developments. Some of the repercussions might be felt for years to come and some might even be irreversible. It is our duty to ensure that we make the right decision so as not to harm future generations.

Conference topics

Biotechnology – risks and responsibility
- *Cloning:* Is cloning right or wrong, moral or immoral? Would it be possible to regulate how far scientists can go?
- *Genetically modified foods:* How do we **weigh up** the benefits and risks? Are GM foods necessary to put an end to world hunger?

The sanctity of life
- *Euthanasia:* Is it not a fundamental human right to decide when the end should come?
- *Abortion:* Should society be permitted to **step in** and **take away** a woman's right to choose?
- *Capital punishment:* Does it act as a deterrent or does it **go against** society's moral obligation to protect life?

The morals of war
- *War:* Can a war be just or should it only be a last resort?
- *Torture in times of terrorism:* Does the end justify the means?

The detailed conference programme will be published shortly. Please fill in the form if you wish to receive more information.

Find the expression which means the same as each phrasal verb.

1. to weigh s.th. up	a) to intervene
2. to step in	b) to remove s.th.
3. to take s.th. away	c) to conflict with s.th.
4. to go against s.th.	d) to consider the importance of two things in relation to one another

Talking about ethics

If "**ethics**" is used to refer to the branch of knowledge that deals with moral principles, it is considered to be singular and is therefore followed by a singular verb, e.g. "Ethics is the study of the values and morals of a person or group of people." *(Ethik)*.

However, if "ethics" is used to refer to the set of moral principles which influence one person's or group of people's actions, then it is treated as plural, e.g. "Sporting ethics are increasingly in the news.".

<u>code</u> of ethics	*Moralkodex*
question of ethics	*Frage der Moral*
ethical issue	*ethische Frage*

in the light of s.th. *(idiom)*	*angesichts einer Sache*	
to become blurred	*verschwimmen*	
to address an issue	*ein Thema ansprechen*	
to raise an issue	*eine Frage aufwerfen*	p. 55
to feel the repercussions of s.th.	*die Auswirkungen einer Sache spüren*	

The word "repercussion" is usually found in the plural and generally refers to unwelcome effects. It is a formal word.

for years to come	*in den kommenden Jahren*
to put an end to s.th. *(idiom)*	*etw. ein Ende machen*
sanctity of life	*die Unantastbarkeit des Lebens*
fundamental human right	*grundlegendes Menschenrecht*
the right to choose	*das Recht frei zu entscheiden*
to act as a deterrent	*zur Abschreckung dienen*
moral obligation	*moralische Verpflichtung*
to be a last resort	*das letzte Mittel sein*
the end justifies the means *(idiom)*	*der Zweck heiligt die Mittel*

<u>in</u> the field of s.th.	*auf dem Gebiet*	
to <u>make</u> the right moral choice	*die richtige moralische Entscheidung treffen*	
public !	*Öffentlichkeit*	p. 131
to <u>make</u> a decision	*eine Entscheidung treffen*	

The opposite of "moral" is "**immoral**". The prefix "im-" is often used to form the opposite of adjectives beginning with "m" and "p", e.g. "mortal" *(sterblich)*, "mature" *(reif)*, "patient" *(geduldig)*, "perfect" *(fehlerfrei, ideal)*, "personal" *(persönlich)*, "polite" *(höflich)*, "possible" *(möglich)*, "probable" *(wahrscheinlich)*, "pure" *(rein)*.

The German word *"Wissenschaftler/in"* is often mistranslated. You only use the word "**scientist**" if you are talking about a natural scientist *(Naturwissenschaftler/in)*. If you mean a specialist in a particular field, then you should use the word "scholar". p. 118

to fill <u>in</u> (a form)	*(ein Formular) ausfüllen*

You can also say "to fill out a form".

Alleviating poverty

In 2006 the Nobel Peace Prize was jointly **awarded** to Muhammad Yunus and Grameen Bank for their innovative work in the area of microcredit – small loans that have helped to lift millions out of **abject poverty** in Bangladesh. The **overwhelming majority of** the people who **take out a loan** are women.

The following is an extract from the presentation speech given by Professor Ole Danbolt Mjøs, the Chairman of the Norwegian Nobel Committee, at the Nobel Prize awards in Oslo on 10 December 2006:

❝ In recent weeks, growing numbers of people **have become acquainted with** the outlines of Yunus's exciting story. Trained in **economics** in the United States, he returned to Bangladesh in 1972 and **took a chair in** economics at the University of Chittagong. In 1974 he **underwent a personal crisis** during the country's famine. **It shook him** to see such poverty. And he asked himself, "What is the point of all these splendid economic theories when people around me are **dying of hunger**?" **As early as** in 1976, he **hit on the idea of** opening a bank for poor people. He **lent** 27 dollars out of his own pocket to 42 craftsmen in a little village in Bangladesh, telling them that they could pay the money back when they could afford to. In the weeks that followed, he **gave the matter a great deal of thought**, and decided that there would have to be an institutional solution.
The result was Grameen Bank, which is present today in the vast majority of Bangladesh's thousands of villages, and which since its formal opening in 1983 has lent almost six billion dollars. Today the bank has almost seven million borrowers. Grameen Bank lends 800 million dollars **per year** in loans, each averaging just over one hundred dollars. The bank is self-financing and **makes a profit**. The repayment percentage is very high. Muhammad Yunus says, "Lend the poor money in amounts which suit them, teach them a few sound financial principles, and they manage on their own."

Everyone has both the potential and the right to live a **decent** life. Mr Yunus has tried to transform the **vicious circle** of "low-income, low saving and low investment", helping the needy to **escape poverty** and **be financially independent**. He believes that **bridging the gap between** rich and poor countries is **crucial to** reducing conflict around the world. His vision is to **eliminate poverty** in the world **in the long-term**. ❞

Talking about poverty

to live in abject ['æbdʒekt] **poverty**	*in entsetzlicher Armut leben*
to live below the poverty line	*unter der Armutsgrenze leben*
to live on the breadline *(idiom)*	*an der Armutsgrenze leben*
to escape poverty	*der Armut entkommen*
to be poverty-stricken	*bettelarm sein*
to eliminate poverty	*die Armut ausrotten*
to reduce poverty	*die Armut verringern*
to combat / tackle poverty	*die Armut bekämpfen*
to alleviate [ə'liːvɪeɪt] poverty	*die Armut lindern*

Talking about lending and borrowing

If you "**lend**" someone something, you give it to them and they will give it back. So they borrow it. Banks lend money. This money is called a loan.

to take out a loan	*ein Darlehen aufnehmen*
to pay interest <u>on</u> a loan	*Zinsen für ein Darlehen bezahlen*
to pay off / back a loan	*ein Darlehen zurückzahlen*
to charge interest (<u>on</u> a loan)	*Zinsen berechnen (für einen Kredit)*

The word "interest" is singular and there is no plural.

The verb "to loan" is a synonym for "to lend".
If something is "on loan" it means it has been lent to someone, e.g. "The book is out on loan.".

to award s.o. a prize	*jdm. einen Preis verleihen*
the overwhelming / vast majority of	*die überwiegende Mehrheit*
to become acquainted with s.th.	*mit etw. vertraut werden*
to become acquainted with s.o.	*eine Bekanntschaft mit jdm. schließen*
to take a chair in s.th. (at a university)	*einen Lehrstuhl (an einer Universität) übernehmen*
to undergo a personal crisis	*eine persönliche Krise durchmachen*
to shake s.o. (up) *(fig.)*	*jdn. aufwühlen*
to hit on an idea	*eine Idee haben*
to give s.th. a great deal of thought	*viel über etw. nachdenken*
to make a profit	*einen Gewinn erzielen*
vicious ['vɪʃəs] **circle** *(idiom)*	*Teufelskreis*
to be financially independent	*finanziell unabhängig sein*
to bridge the gap between *(idiom)*	*die Kluft überbrücken zwischen*

economics	*Wirtschaftslehre*	p. 124
to <u>die of</u> hunger	*verhungern*	
as early <u>as</u>	*schon, bereits*	
<u>per</u> year	*pro Jahr*	
decent ['diːsnt] **!**	*anständig*	
to be crucial <u>to</u> s.th.	*für etw. entscheidend sein*	
<u>in</u> the long-term	*langfristig*	

51

Famous US philanthropists

Andrew Carnegie embodied the American Dream – he was an immigrant who **went from rags to riches**, **making his fortune** in the steel business. In his essay "The Gospel of Wealth", he wrote that the rich should not **throw money around**, but should provide moderately for their families, and distribute the rest of their wealth to promote the welfare and happiness of other people. He believed that "a man who dies rich, dies disgraced". He **followed his own advice** and instead of **living in the lap of luxury**, **gave away** nearly **$350 million** or almost 90 percent of his money to a variety of **good causes**.

John D. Rockefeller was born in 1839 and grew up on a farm **in modest circumstances**. He **made his money in** oil, founding the Standard Oil Company. A devout Baptist, from 1897 onwards **he devoted himself** to philanthropy. He **set up** several important foundations and **donated** a total of $540 million to charitable purposes. His son, the **heir to the Rockefeller fortune**, **carried on** his father's philanthropic work.

Warren Buffett is generally considered to be the world's most successful investor. By the time he was 17 he had bought his first share and **made enough money** from delivering newspapers to buy agricultural land and rent it to farmers. Despite being the world's second richest man (Forbes list 2006), Buffett **has modest tastes** and does not **splash out on** many luxuries. In fact, in June 2006 he made the greatest charitable gift in history **to date** by **pledging** the **bulk of his** then over $40 billion **fortune** to the **Bill and Melinda Gates** Foundation. He said of his decision, "We agreed with Andrew Carnegie, who said that huge fortunes that flow **in large part** from society should in large part be returned to society."

Find the expression on the right which means the same as each phrasal verb on the left.

1. *to give s.th. away*	a) *to found s.th.*
2. *to set s.th. up*	b) *to continue s.th.*
3. *to carry s.th. on*	c) *to let s.o. have s.th. for free*

Talking about money

to **throw** money **around** *(idiom)*	*mit Geld um sich werfen*
to **make** one's money **in** s.th.	*sein Geld mit etw. verdienen*
to **donate** money	*Geld spenden*
to **make** money	*Geld verdienen*
to waste money	*Geld verschwenden*
to spend money <u>on</u> s.th.	*Geld für etw. ausgeben*
to save money, *also:* to save up	*Geld sparen*
to be short of money	*knapp bei Kasse sein*

Talking about being rich or poor

to have lots of money	to be well-off
	to be well-heeled *(inf., idiom)*
	to be rolling in it *(inf.)*
to have little money	to be badly-off
	money is tight *(inf.)*
to have no money	to be flat broke *(inf., idiom)*
	to be penniless
to make ends meet *(inf., idiom)*	*über die Runden kommen*
to tighten one's belt *(inf., idiom)*	*den Gürtel enger schnallen*
to **go from rags to riches** *(idiom)*	*vom Tellerwäscher zum Millionär werden*
to **make** one's **fortune**	*ein Vermögen machen*
to **follow** s.o.'s **advice**	*jds. Ratschlag folgen*
to **live in the lap of luxury** *(idiom)*	*ein Luxusleben führen*
to lead a life of luxury	
good cause	*guter Zweck*
to **grow up in modest circumstances**	*in bescheidenen Verhältnissen aufwachsen*
to **devote** o.s. **to** s.th.	*sich etw. widmen*
to **have modest tastes**	*bescheiden sein*
to have expensive tastes	*einen teuren Geschmack haben*

Note, in these expressions the word "taste" is always in the plural.

to **pledge** s.th. **to** s.o.	*jdm. etw. zusichern*
the bulk of one's fortune	*der größte Teil des Vermögens*

$350 million – Remember in English there is no gap between the currency symbol and the amount.

to **be heir** [ɛə] <u>to</u> s.o.'s **fortune**	*jds. Vermögen erben*
to **splash out** <u>on</u> s.th.	*Geld für etw. hinauswerfen*
<u>to</u> **date** *(formal)*	*bis heute*
<u>in</u> **large part**	*zum größten Teil*

A global world

Presenter: Good evening and welcome to tonight's discussion on globalization, a word that seems to **be on everyone's lips** nowadays. But what does it actually mean and what changes has it **brought about**?

Guest 1: **For better or worse**, globalization **touches our lives** in ways that most of us never stop to think about. In the past it was often seen as a process that **created new economic opportunities** by removing **trade barriers**, but that's only the **tip of the iceberg**. The most obvious ways it has **affected** us are the changes in communication, technology and transport.

Guest 2: It also allows poor countries and their citizens to **seize opportunities** and to **raise *their* standard of living**. And better communications have also furthered our understanding.

Guest 3: Now let's not **get carried away** – it hasn't made the world a more peaceful place by removing local tensions or conflicts – it's merely **brought** them **to our attention**. And new technologies are actually also **sweeping away** cultural boundaries. Global entertainment companies **have a lot to answer for** as they generally promote Western **consumer culture at the expense of** local cultures. This **is also true of** multinational corporations who have **set up** subsidiaries around the world without always being **sensitive to** local customs.

Guest 4: I quite agree! And **let's face it**, globalization also **raises some other very serious issues**. Our increasingly borderless world is making it more difficult to fight crime and terrorism, **not to mention** the **spread of infectious diseases**. Nowadays, no country **is immune to** the **threat posed** by an isolated outbreak of an infectious disease.

Which expression means the same as each of these phrasal verbs?

1. to bring s.th. about	*a) to found s.th.*
2. to sweep s.th. away	*b) to make s.th. happen*
3. to set s.th. up	*c) to get rid of s.th.*

Talking about opportunities

to create new opportunities	*neue Chancen eröffnen*
to seize [siːz] **an opportunity**	*eine Gelegenheit ergreifen*
to make the most of an opportunity	*das Beste aus einer Gelegenheit machen*
to take the opportunity to do s.th.	*die Gelegenheit nutzen, etw. zu tun*
a golden opportunity	*eine einmalige Gelegenheit*

Talking about issues

An "issue" ['ɪʃuː] is an important topic that people discuss and often relates to society or politics. Do not confuse it with the word "theme" (main idea). p. 190

to raise an issue	*ein Thema aufwerfen*
to address an issue	*ein Thema ansprechen*
to avoid an issue	*ein Thema vermeiden*
burning / controversial issue	*brennendes / kontroverses Thema*

However if "someone has issues", it means that they have problems.

to be on everyone's lips *(idiom)*	*in aller Munde sein*
for better or worse *(idiom)*	*hier: so oder so*

This phrase also occurs in a traditional marriage ceremony when the couple promises to stay together in good and in bad times.

to touch s.o.'s life	*jds. Leben berühren*
trade barriers	*Handelsbarrieren*
the tip of the iceberg *(idiom)*	*die Spitze des Eisbergs*
to raise s.o.'s standard of living	*jds. Lebensstandard erhöhen*
to get carried away *(inf.)*	*es übertreiben*
to bring s.th. to s.o.'s attention	*jds. Aufmerksamkeit auf etw. lenken*
to have a lot to answer for	*einiges auf dem Kerbholz haben*
let's face it *also:* let's be honest	*seien wir ehrlich*
not to mention *(idiom)*	*geschweige denn*
the spread of disease	*Ausbreitung von Krankheit*
infectious disease	*ansteckende Krankheit*
to pose a threat	*eine Bedrohung darstellen*

The verbs "**to affect**" and "**to effect**" are often confused.
"To affect" is the more commonly used verb and means to influence, e.g. "Drinking alcohol can affect your ability to drive a car.".
"To effect" is a formal word and means to successfully cause or bring about, e.g. "Building was stopped until repairs were effected.".
The noun is spelt "effect" and means result or consequence. p. 108

consumer culture	*Konsumkultur*
at the expense of s.th.	*auf Kosten von etw.*
to be true of s.th.	*zutreffend sein für etw.*
sensitive to s.th.	*sensibel (genug) für etw.*
to be immune to s.th.	*immun sein gegen etw.*

Science-fiction films

Do you know which science-fiction films they are?

1. An entrepreneur has **come up with** an unusual idea for a theme park: live dinosaurs. Scientists have developed a way of bringing dinosaurs to life, using genetic code (DNA) taken from dinosaur blood, preserved inside fossilized mosquitoes. Before the park opens, two dinosaur specialists, a mathematician and the owner's two grandchildren are given a tour of the park. But when the security system **breaks down**, the dinosaurs are able to **break out of** their enclosures ... One of the first films to use CGI, it revolutionized the film industry.

2. The polar ice caps have melted and all of the coastal cities are underwater. However, the human race is advancing fast – man has succeeded in creating realistic robots, called mechas. One mecha company produces an artificial child, David, who has realistic feelings. He is adopted by a family whose real son has an incurable disease. However, after some time a cure is discovered and the son returns home, changing David's life dramatically. The film, set in the near and distant future, looks at what it means to be human and the meaning of humanity.

3. Thomas Anderson works for a computer software company and does some hacking on the side. However, his world soon turns upside down when he is contacted by a man who tells him that his world is actually only a simulated reality. The real world has been laid waste and **taken over** by an advanced artificial intelligence system. It has **tapped into** people's minds and created the illusion of a real world while it uses their brains and bodies as a source of energy to feed the system. Now it is up to Anderson and others to try to overthrow the machines. The film made use of groundbreaking special effects.

Which expression means the same as these phrasal verbs?

1. to come up with s.th.	*a) to suddenly stop functioning*
2. to break down	*b) to take control of s.th.*
3. to break out of s.th.	*c) to think of s.th. (such as a plan or an idea)*
4. to take s.th. over	*d) to penetrate s.th.*
5. to tap into s.th.	*e) to escape from s.th.*

Answers: p. 201

Talking about humans

The word "**human**" refers to people *(menschlich)*.

It is also used formally to refer to being human (rather than an animal or object), e.g. "The archaeologists found human and animal remains.".

the human race	*die Menschheit*

"The human race" does not have a plural. It is synonymous with "mankind" although the former is often preferred as it is neutral.　p. 196

human being	*Mensch*
human nature	*die menschliche Natur*

In English "human nature" does not have an article.

The Human Genome Project	*Projekt zur Erforschung der menschlichen Gene*

The word "**humane**" [hjuːˈmeɪn] means having or showing compassion, e.g. "Prisoners have the right to humane treatment." *(human)*.

The word "**humanity**" refers to the human race, e.g. "Nuclear weapons are a threat to humanity.".

"Humanity" also describes the quality of being humane, e.g. "She treated them with great care and humanity.".

to bring s.th. (back) to life	*etw. (wieder) zum Leben erwecken*
genetic code	*genetischer Code*
gene [dʒiːn] test	*Gentest*
to give s.o. a tour of s.th.	*jdm. herumführen*
to turn s.th. upside down *(idiom)*	*etw. auf den Kopf stellen*
to lay waste to s.th. *(idiom)*	*etw. verwüsten*
artificial intelligence	*künstliche Intelligenz*
to be up to s.o. to do s.th.	*jds. Aufgabe sein, etw. zu tun*
groundbreaking special effects	*bahnbrechende Spezialeffekte*

scientist	*Wissenschaftler/in*	p. 118
DN<u>A</u> (= deoxyribonucleic acid)	*DNS (= Desoxyribonukleinsäure)*	
specialist (<u>in</u> s.th.)	*Spezialist/in für etw.*	

In English "specialist" has an article, e.g. "She's <u>a</u> computer specialist.".

CGI (= computer generated imagery)	*Computeranimation*
to succeed in do<u>ing</u> s.th.	*etw. mit Erfolg tun*
to succeed <u>in</u> s.th.	*mit etw. Erfolg haben*
to have an <u>in</u>curable [ɪnˈkjʊərəbl] **disease**	*eine unheilbare Krankheit haben*
to discover a cure (<u>for</u> s.th.)	*ein Mittel gegen eine Krankheit finden*
to cure s.o. <u>of</u> a disease	*jdn. von einer Krankheit heilen*

The word "cure" also means a solution to a problem, e.g. "Some people believe that debt relief is the cure for poverty." *(Mittel gegen Armut)*.

on the side *(idiom)*	*nebenbei*

1. **Choose the correct preposition to complete each of these sentences. Each preposition may only be used once.**

> at – for – in – in – in – of – on – per – to – to – with

1. _____ average, I get fifty e-mails _____ day – most of which are spam.

2. A cure _____ the common cold has still not been discovered.

3. He was charged _____ disturbing the peace.

4. The UN said in a press release that around 18,000 children die _____ hunger and malnutrition every day.

5. This is the artist's best work _____ date, _____ large part due to his inventive use of colour.

6. Children and those with respiratory problems are more sensitive _____ ozone. People who work outdoors are also _____ risk.

7. He's a specialist _____ environmental law.

8. Ten people were killed _____ the blast.

2. **Combine a word on the left with one on the right to find euphemisms to do with war. Then give their direct meaning in English.**

body	damage	_____
collateral	fire	_____
friendly	target	_____
soft	count	_____

3. "Human", "humane" or "humanity"? Complete these sentences using the correct word.

1. The _____ brain is very complex.

2. Global warming poses a great threat to _____.

3. This food is unfit for _____ consumption.

4. They are campaigning for the _____ treatment of farm animals.

5. _____ describes the quality of being kind or _____.

6. I wonder if the _____ race will ever populate another planet?

7. The expression _____ rights refers to the basic rights which every _____ being should have.

4. Which expression is the odd one out in each case?

1. ❑ to blow up   ❑ to go off   ❑ to break out

2. ❑ to wage war   ❑ to avert war   ❑ to fight a war

3. ❑ to be rolling in it   ❑ to be penniless   ❑ to be broke

4. ❑ to have issues   ❑ to raise an issue   ❑ to address an issue

5. ❑ to spend money   ❑ to donate money   ❑ to give away money

6. ❑ to combat poverty   ❑ to tackle poverty   ❑ to alleviate poverty

7. ❑ to borrow money   ❑ to lend money   ❑ to take out a loan

8. ❑ to affect   ❑ to influence   ❑ to effect

5. **Rewrite these sentences using the phrasal verbs below. Don't forget to use the verb in the right tense!**

> to bring about – to come up with s.th. – to die out –
> to give o.s. up – to pull s.o. over – to set s.th. up –
> to weigh up

1. The police ordered him to stop his car.

   _____

2. He allowed himself to be arrested.

   _____

3. Forty years ago, he thought of a good idea and founded his own business. *(Replace both expressions with phrasal verbs!)*

   _____

   _____

4. Many plant and animal species are becoming extinct as a result of global warming.

   _____

   _____

5. We need to consider the pros and cons of cloning before we make a decision.

   _____

   _____

6. Global warming has already begun to cause changes in the weather around the world.

   _____

   _____

6. **Match the idioms on the left to their meaning on the right. Then put the correct idiom into each sentence.**

1. to be in the same boat	a) in order to achieve a goal it is all right to do something bad
2. to go from bad to worse	b) a small part of a problem which is really much larger than it seems
3. vicious circle	c) to spend less money than you used to because you have less to spend
4. to tighten one's belt	d) to be in the same difficult situation as others
5. the tip of the iceberg	e) a difficult situation that cannot be solved because it causes another problem which in turn causes the first one again
6. the end justifies the means	f) to get worse than it already is

1. Everything started going _____ – one of the detergents used to clean up the oil spill caused more damage to wildlife than the oil itself.

2. We are all _____ and must act together to protect our environment.

3. Business has not been very good recently, so I think we'll all have to _____.

4. We'll have to cut down these trees to build the new swimming pool – well, I suppose _____.

5. It's a _____ – the more we give, the more people start to expect.

6. A few cases of bird flu have been reported, but we think it's just

_____.

Job satisfaction – a novel

Chapter One

Saunders was sitting at his desk lost in thought and staring blankly at the calendar on the wall. Suddenly he sighed and turned his attention back to the note lying in front of him.

Need launch plan asap. Lewis

The problem was that he hated being stuck behind a desk. He couldn't face writing another plan for a product in which he didn't believe. It hadn't always been like that. When he'd **started out** twelve years ago, he'd quickly made a name for himself because he'd never been on sick leave, had hardly ever taken time off, had never missed a deadline and had **come up with** some of the company's most successful marketing strategies. He'd **stuck at it**, starting at the bottom doing placements in a variety of companies and steadily climbing up the career ladder. Now he was a senior marketing executive with a very high-powered job. But for some time he'd had itchy feet.

And then it happened. He got up, marched into Lewis' office and simply announced "I quit".
Lewis looked at him aghast then said, "You can't just come in here and resign. What on earth's wrong with you? What's going on?"
Saunders glared at him and said "I've had enough! I'm burnt out and I'm finally going to do something I've always dreamed of doing."
"And what's that?" asked Lewis.
"I'm going to be a private investigator."
And with that, Saunders turned around and walked out of the room, leaving his startled boss staring after him.
...

Which expression means the same as each of these phrasal verbs?

1. to start out	*a) to think of s.th.*
2. to come up with s.th.	*b) to persevere with s.th.*
3. to stick at s.th.	*c) to begin s.th.*

Talking about jobs

"Work" is an uncountable noun, e.g. "It's not always easy to find work." but "job" is countable, e.g. "I've got a new job.". In English you "<u>do</u> a job / <u>do</u> work".

high-powered		*anspruchsvolle Arbeit*
steady		*fester Arbeitsplatz*
nine-to-five	**job**	*Achtstundentag*
part-time		*Halbtagsstelle*
dead-end		*Beruf ohne Zukunft*

job satisfaction	*Zufriedenheit am Arbeitsplatz*	
to be lost in thought *(idiom)*	*tief in Gedanken versunken sein*	
to hate being stuck behind a desk	*Schreibtischarbeit hassen*	
to not be able to face (doing) s.th.	*sich nicht zu etw. durchringen können*	
to be on sick leave	*krankgeschrieben sein*	p. 126
to take time off	*sich freinehmen*	

"Off" is used to talk about times away from work, e.g. "Can I have Monday off?". In English we do not talk about a "free day", we talk about a "day off".

to start at the bottom	*unten anfangen*
to climb up the career ladder *(idiom)*	*die Karriereleiter aufsteigen*
to have itchy feet *(idiom)*	*hier: sich nach etw. Neuem sehnen*
to quit a job *(inf.)*	*kündigen*
What on earth...? *(inf.)*	*Was zum Teufel...?*
What's going on? *(inf.)*	*Was geht hier vor?*
to be burnt out *(inf.)*	*völlig ausgebrannt sein*
and with that	*hier: mit diesen Worten*

A "**calendar**" usually has pictures and hangs on the wall. You write down appointments in a "diary" *(Terminkalender)* or an "organizer".

to turn one's attention <u>to</u> s.th.	*seine Aufmerksamkeit auf etw. richten*	
note !	*Notiz*	p. 132

"**asap**" is short for "as soon as possible". Be careful, the letters are always pronounced separately, i.e. "A, S, A, P", and not as one word.

to believe <u>in</u> s.th.	*an etw. glauben*
to make a name <u>for</u> o.s.	*sich einen Namen machen*
to miss a deadline	*einen Termin nicht einhalten*
to meet a deadline	*einen Termin einhalten*

There are different translations for the German word *"Termin"*. A "deadline" is the latest date or time by which something should be done. An "appointment" is an arrangement to meet someone at a specific time and place.

p. 118

to <u>do</u> a placement *(AE internship)*	
to <u>go on</u> (a) placement	*ein Praktikum machen*
to <u>do</u> work experience	

After work

Robert: Sorry I'm late – I **was tied up** at the office. My boss organized a meeting **at the last minute** and it **went on** for ages.

Andy: So how's the new job going? **Found your feet** yet?

Robert: Sort of. It's just really busy at the moment. One of my colleagues **handed in his notice** last week – he's **accepted a job offer** in the States. The problem is, he's leaving at the end of the month as he's got so much **overtime**. That means we'll be **one person short** in the team until we get his replacement. And we've got a major presentation **coming up** so I'**m up to my ears** at the moment! Anyway, what about you?

Andy: Everything's fine! I'**m at a bit of a loose end** at the moment as we've just finished one project and the next one hasn't started. But I'm not complaining – it's nice not to have my boss **breathing down my neck** and to be able to **knock off** early once in a while. Did I tell you, Jane's working for us now? She'**s standing in for** Mary who's **on maternity leave**.

Robert: That's great! I'm sure she'll **do a good job** – she's got loads of experience. By the way, did you hear about Sean? He was **made redundant** last month – apparently the company's profits are down and so they started **laying off** people in his department.

Andy: How's he **taking it**?

Robert: He's actually quite happy about the whole thing because he's now decided to **go freelance** so that he can work more flexible hours.

Which expression means the same as each of these phrasal verbs?

1. to go on	*a) to do s.o. else's job while they are not available*
2. to come up	*b) to last*
3. to stand in for s.o.	*c) to be about to happen soon*

Talking about being busy

to be tied up *(inf., idiom)*	*beschäftigt sein*
to be up to one's ears in s.th. *(inf., idiom)*	*bis über die Ohren in Arbeit stecken*

You can also say "to be up to one's eyes / eyeballs in s.th.".

to be snowed under (with work)	*in Arbeit ersticken*
to be at a loose end *(inf., idiom)*	*nicht wissen, was man mit sich anfangen soll*

Talking about changing jobs

to hand in one's notice	*seine Kündigung einreichen*
to give s.o. his / her notice	*jdm. die Kündigung aussprechen*

Remember, the word "notice" also refers to an official sign giving news or information that is placed in a prominent position so that everyone will see (or notice) it. It has nothing to do with the German word *"Notiz"* which means "note".

p. 132

to resign (from a job)	*(einen Job) kündigen*
to hand in one's resignation	*seine Kündigung einreichen*
to be made redundant	*den Arbeitsplatz verlieren*
to lay s.o. off *(inf.)*	*jdn. entlassen*
to fire s.o. *(inf.)* / to sack s.o. *(BE, inf.)*	*jdn. rausschmeißen*

If you "lay people off", you end their employment (sometimes temporarily) because you do not have any work for them. However, if you "fire" or "sack" someone, it is generally because the person has done something wrong or his or her work is not good. If you "get the sack", you are fired.

to find one's feet *(inf., idiom)*	*Fuß fassen*
to accept a job (offer)	*eine Stelle annehmen*
to apply for a job	*sich für eine Stelle bewerben*
to offer s.o. a job	*jdm. eine Stelle anbieten*
to be one person short	*es fehlt eine Person*
to breathe down s.o.'s neck *(inf., idiom)*	*jdm. im Nacken sitzen*
to knock off (work) *(inf.)*	*Feierabend machen*
to do a good job	*gute Arbeit leisten*

If you ask how someone "**is taking s.th.**", you want to know what the person's reaction is *(wie er / sie es aufnimmt)*. It is an informal expression.

to go freelance	*freiberuflich tätig werden*

at the last minute	*in letzter Minute*
overtime	*hier: Überstunden*

"Overtime" refers to the extra hours someone works, e.g. "She's done a lot of overtime." as well as to the money that is paid for this *(Überstundenzuschlag)*, e.g. "We do not pay overtime.". In both cases the noun is uncountable.

to be on maternity leave	*in Elternzeit sein (Mütter)*
to be on paternity leave	*in Elternzeit sein (Väter)*

Setting up a business

Are you thinking of starting up on your own or going into business with a partner? Here are a few things you should consider to see if you have what it takes!

Personality	*Yes*	*No*
Are you prepared for the personal demands of running your own business?	☐	☐
Are you prepared to take chances?	☐	☐
Do you have the right kind of personality to go it alone?	☐	☐
Are you determined to succeed?	☐	☐
Are you committed enough to **put in** the long hours to get started?	☐	☐

Business idea		
Have you **looked into** what kind of competition your product or services face?	☐	☐
Have you carried out the necessary market research?	☐	☐
Do you have the skills to **win** people **over to** your ideas?	☐	☐
Have you put together a realistic business plan?	☐	☐

Finances		
Can you accept the loss of benefits such as paid holiday, a company pension scheme, sick pay, etc.?	☐	☐
Will you be able to survive financially until your business has got off the ground?	☐	☐
Do you have sufficient funds to launch your business?	☐	☐

As many people who have started successful businesses will agree, the secret of success is largely dependent on a good idea, thorough planning, your attitude and skills.

Which expression means the same as these phrasal verbs?

1. to put in (hours / work)	*a) to investigate s.th.*
2. to look into s.th.	*b) to spend time doing s.th. or make a particular effort to do s.th.*
3. to win s.o. over (to s.th.)	*c) to persuade s.o. to agree with you*

Talking about business

to set up a business	*ein Geschäft gründen*
to launch [ɔ:] a business	
to start up on one's own	*sich selbstständig machen*
to go into business (with s.o.)	*mit jdm. ein Geschäft gründen*
to set up in business as a lawyer (doctor)	*sich als Rechtsanwalt/anwältin (Arzt/Ärztin) niederlassen*
to run a business	*ein Geschäft führen*

Talking about company benefits

paid holiday	*bezahlte Urlaubstage*
company pension scheme	*betriebliche Altersversorgung*

In English, the word "pension" is used to refer to the regular payment you receive either from the state or from an investment fund when you retire *(Rente)*. When you leave your job because you have reached the retirement age, you "retire" *(in Rente gehen)*.

to be living on a state pension	*von der Staatsrente leben*	
sick pay	*Krankengeld*	p. 126
paid sick leave	*bezahlte Krankheitstage*	

to have what it takes (to do s.th.)	*das Zeug dazu haben, etw. zu tun*
to be prepared for s.th.	*auf etw. vorbereitet sein*
to be prepared to do s.th.	*bereit sein, etw. zu tun*
to go it alone *(inf., idiom)*	*im Alleingang handeln*
to be determined to do s.th.	*fest entschlossen sein, etw. zu tun*
to face competition	*dem Wettbewerb ausgesetzt sein*
to carry out (market) research	*(Markt-) Forschung betreiben*
to do (market) research	
to conduct (market) research *(formal)*	
to get s.th. off the ground *(inf., idiom)*	*etw. realisieren*
to have sufficient funds	*genügend Kapital haben*

The word "funds" is used in the plural when it means financial resources *(Geldmittel)*. It is often used together with the word "public", e.g. "Public funds should not be used for private institutions." *(öffentliche Mittel)*. A "fund" is a sum of money made available for a particular purpose *(Fonds)*.

to set up a fund	*einen Fonds einrichten*
to fund s.th.	*etw. finanzieren*
the secret of success	*Schlüssel zum Erfolg*

to be dependent on s.th.	*von etw. abhängen*

Take care when writing the word "dependent". If you see it written with an "a" ("dependant"), it is a noun and refers to a person who is financially dependent on someone else, usually a family member *(Abhängige/r)*. However, the noun is increasingly being spelt the same way as the adjective.

Travel tips: a gap year

So you've decided to **take the plunge** and want to see a bit of the world before you do something else? Here are a few tips to help you **make the most of** your gap year.

- Of course first of all you have to decide where to go and what to do. Whether you decide to work full-time, **do voluntary work** or **go backpacking**, will partly **depend on** your budget. Volunteering is becoming increasingly popular as it is a way of being a responsible tourist, getting to know the **locals**, and putting something back. Teaching English in China, **doing conservation work** in Ecuador, building a school in Tanzania – these are just a few of the things you can do.

- Check up to see if you need to **get any jabs** before you go. Also ask your doctor about any medicines you should take with you.

- You might need a visa to travel and work in some countries. Make sure to allow plenty of time when you **apply for** it. And remember to check whether your **passport is going to expire** while you're away.

- **Take out decent travel insurance** – make sure it covers everything that you're planning to do (you might need extra cover for some sporting activities).

- It's advisable to book **accommodation** for the first two nights so that you can get to know **the lie of the land**.

- **Travel light**! Just remember you'll have to carry your backpack so think really carefully about what you're packing. And remember, you can always buy things when you'**re on the road** – it's often cheaper.

- Decide on how you're going to **keep in touch with** everyone **back home** (maybe online, **mobile phone**, letter).

Here's what people have said about their gap experiences:

Jane, 19: "Fantastic – I saw parts of Tanzania I would never have seen as a typical tourist but more importantly I gave something back to the **local community**."

Jim, 20: "I went backpacking round New Zealand – it was a brilliant way to **recharge my batteries** before starting university!"

Talking about travelling

to go backpacking	*mit dem Rucksack reisen*
to travel light *(idiom)*	*mit wenig Gepäck reisen*
to be on the road *(idiom)*	*unterwegs sein*
gap year *(BE)*	*hier: das Jahr zwischen Schule und Universität*
to take / have a gap year = to have a year off / out	*ein Jahr aussetzen*
to take the plunge *(idiom)*	*den Schritt wagen*
to make the most of s.th.	*etw. ausnutzen*
to do voluntary work = to volunteer	*ehrenamtlich tätig sein*
to do conservation work	*sich aktiv für den Naturschutz engagieren*
to get a jab *(inf.)* to be vaccinated against s.th.	*(gegen etw.) geimpft werden*

If your passport "**expires**" *(ablaufen)*, it runs out and is no longer valid. It is an official word.

to take out insurance (against s.th.)	*eine Versicherung (gegen etw.) abschließen*

"Insurance" is uncountable. An "insurance policy" is the written agreement between a person and the insurance company which contains all the details.

the lie of the land *(idiom)* *also:* the lay of the land	*die Lage*
to keep in touch with s.o. *(idiom)*	*mit jdm. in Kontakt bleiben*

You can also say "to stay in touch with s.o.". If you "are in touch with s.o.", you are in regular contact with them.

back home = at home	*zu Hause*
to recharge one's batteries *(idiom)*	*neue Kräfte tanken*
to depend <u>on</u> s.th.	*von etw. abhängen*

If "**local**" ['ləʊkl] is used as a noun, it refers to a person who lives in a particular place rather than a visitor *(Einheimischer)*. When it is used as an adjective, it refers to something from a particular area that is usually found exclusively there, e.g. "**the local community**" *(die hiesige Gemeinde)*. If British people talk about their "local", it is an informal way of talking about the pub to which they go near their home *(Stammkneipe)*.

to apply for a <u>visa</u>	*ein Visum beantragen*

Remember, the English word ends with an "a"!

decent ['diːsnt] **!**	*hier: angemessen*

Even native speakers often misspell the word "**accommodation**" – there are two "c's" and two "m's"! And it is an uncountable noun, so you cannot use "an" or put it in the plural. However, in *AE* you can use the plural.

British talk about their "**mobile phone**" or "mobile" *(Handy)*. In the US people talk about their "cell phone" or "cell".

Back from holiday

Amy: Hi Steve, welcome back! How was your holiday?

Steve: Really relaxing! Jane and I **went self-catering** in the south of France. She'd wanted to **go camping** again, but I really **couldn't face it** so **in the end** we **reached a compromise** and rented a little place down near Grasse. It was right **in the middle of nowhere** and a great place to **chill out**. I have to admit we didn't really do much – spent time at the beach, visited some very **picturesque** villages, went on some **scenic drives** and spent a day in Cannes. How was your **trip to** the States?

Amy: Well it didn't **start off** too well – in fact the **journey** there was a complete nightmare! Our plane was delayed for six hours and so we missed our connecting flight and spent a miserable night in some **run-down hotel** near the airport. Well anyway, **to cut a long story short**, when we finally reached San Francisco things did begin to **look up**! The weather was absolutely fantastic. We spent two nights in San Francisco, went hiking in the national parks for a few days and then went south along the coast to LA. It's a very beautiful drive – the scenery is **breathtaking**.

Steve: We were there several years ago and really enjoyed it, too. I'd love to go back there one day. Where did you stay?

Amy: We decided not to **rough it** this time and stayed in B&Bs. By the way, guess who we **ran into** in San Francisco? An old schoolfriend of yours – Jeremy Spencer! It's **a small world**, isn't it? He asked **to be remembered to you**.

Which expression on the right means the same as each of these phrasal verbs?

1. *to chill out	a) to start a journey
2. to start off	b) to meet s.o. by chance
3. to look up	c) to relax
4. to run into s.o.	d) to start improving

Talking about holidays

The word "**holiday**" is usually in the singular, unless you are referring to more than one holiday, e.g. "He went to France on holiday." but "He spent his last three holidays in France.". In the US, the word "vacation" is used.

to go on holiday / to take a holiday	*Urlaub machen*
to be on holiday	*Urlaub haben*
to have a two-week holiday / to have two weeks' holiday	*zwei Wochen in Urlaub fahren*
to need a holiday	*Urlaub / Ferien brauchen*

The above expressions are not used in the plural. However, you talk about the "school holidays", "the Easter holidays", "the summer holidays".
In the UK a "bank holiday" is a "public holiday" *(Feiertag)*; in the US, people talk about a "holiday" or "public holiday". In the US the "holidays" refer to the time around Christmas and New Year.

Talking about trips

If you go away on a short holiday or for business, this is usually referred to as a "**trip**", e.g. "He has gone on a business trip.", "Have a good trip!".
A "**journey**" is a trip from one place to another. A "**drive**" is a trip in which you travel by car.
A "voyage" is used to describe a long journey by sea or in space, e.g. "Darwin went on a famous voyage to South America.".
A "ride" is a short trip you make in a car, or on a bus, bike or motorbike.
Your "travels" refers to the journeys you make, usually a long way from home, e.g. "He encountered different cultures on his travels.". p. 122

to go on a voyage, trip, journey	*eine Reise machen*

Talking about scenery

Adjectives that are often used to describe scenery are "**picturesque**" *(malerisch)*, "**breathtaking**" *(atemberaubend)*, "stunning", "spectacular", "magnificent" *(alle drei in etwa: umwerfend)*, "dramatic" *(dramatisch)*.
If something is "**scenic**", it has beautiful views of nature *(landschaftlich schön)*, e.g. "The drive was very scenic.".

to go self-catering	*selbst verpflegen*
to go camping	*zelten gehen*
to not be able to face s.th.	*sich außerstande sehen, etw. zu tun*
to reach a compromise	*zu einem Kompromiss gelangen*
in the middle of nowhere *(idiom)*	*am Ende der Welt*
run-down hotel	*heruntergekommenes Hotel*
to cut a long story short *(idiom)*	*langer Rede kurzer Sinn*
to rough it *(inf.)*	*hier: ohne jeglichen Komfort reisen*
It's a small world! *(idiom)*	*Die Welt ist klein!*
to remember s.o. to s.o.	*jdn. von jdm. grüßen*
in the end	*zum Schluss*

What's on at the leisure centre?

We **have a wide range of** activities **on offer** to help you **get into shape** and stay fit. Whatever your level of fitness, ability, age or interests, **there's something here for everyone**.

- We run over 20 different **exercise classes** a week – from high energy classes like **aerobics** which will help you to **work up a sweat** and burn unwanted calories, to relaxation classes, with specially designed **exercises** to help reduce stress and increase your flexibility.

- Swimming is a great way to improve fitness and to **tone up your muscles**. It's low-impact so you **run less risk of injury**. We have a 25 metre indoor pool with six lanes and a heated outdoor pool which is open **all year round**.

- We have six outdoor all weather **tennis courts**, and six indoor ones. Our professional coaches can help you to **improve your game** – either in individual lessons or group sessions. And if you **feel up to it**, you can **also take part in** the centre's annual tennis tournament.

- Our **athletics** track is the perfect place to train **under the watchful eye of** our experienced coaches.

- We have fully qualified personal trainers who are always **on hand** to give you advice and to help you **achieve your goals**.

Liverpool vs Chelsea

The match got off to a really exciting start. Chelsea **went into the lead** after only six minutes and **scored two more goals** by half-time. It was devastating for Liverpool – they **were 3-0 down**! But then everything changed. Liverpool scored their first goal at the beginning of the second half. And then they scored two more **in quick succession** to equalize. The atmosphere was electric. And then, just before the whistle blew, Liverpool went on to score another goal. The fans **went wild**! **What a match**!

"Oi – change that to Chelsea."

Talking about exercising

to get into shape	*sich in Form bringen*
exercise class	*Fitnessklasse*
to work up a sweat [e]	*ins Schwitzen kommen*
to tone up one's muscles ['mʌslz]	*seine Muskeln kräftigen*

The word "exercise" is used to talk about physical activity in general
(Bewegung), e.g. "Exercise is good for you.". "**Exercises**" in the plural refer
to a task or activity done to test a skill *(Übung)*. In a sporting context
"exercises" means *Gymnastik*, e.g. "I've just done my morning exercises.".
If you "exercise", you do a physical activity in order to stay fit and make
your body stronger *(trainieren)*.

to run the risk of injury	*Gefahr laufen, sich zu verletzen*

What's on?	*Was ist los?*
a wide range of s.th.	*eine Vielfalt an etw.*
to have s.th. on offer	*etw. anbieten*
There's something for everyone!	*Es gibt für jeden etwas!*
all year round	*das ganze Jahr durch*

The German word *"Platz"* has different translations in English: a tennis
<u>court</u>, a golf <u>course</u>, a football <u>pitch</u>, or a playing <u>field</u> *(Sportplatz)*.

to improve one's game	*sein Spiel verbessern*

The general word for *"Spiel"* is "**game**", e.g. "a game of cards", "a game of
football". If the British are talking about an official contest, they use the
word "**match**", e.g. "Did you see the match on TV last night?". However,
the Americans use the word "game", e.g. "We saw the game on TV.".

to feel up to s.th.	*sich etw. gewachsen fühlen*
under the watchful eye of s.o.	*unter jds. wachsamen Auge*
to be on hand *(idiom)*	*hier: zur Verfügung stehen*
to achieve one's goal	*sein Ziel erreichen*
to go into the lead [liːd]	*die Führung übernehmen*
to score a goal	*ein Tor schießen*
to be 3-0 down	*3:0 zurückliegen*

In sport "0" is pronounced "nil", except in tennis when it is called "love". p. 178

in quick succession	*schnell hintereinander*
to go wild *(inf.)*	*ausflippen*

Like "**aerobics**", "**athletics**" is a plural noun that is usually treated as being
singular (and so followed by a singular verb), e.g. "Athletics refers to sports
that involve running, jumping and throwing.". p. 134

to <u>do</u> aerobic<u>s</u>	*Aerobik machen*
to take part <u>in</u> s.th.	*an etw. teilnehmen*
vs (= versus)	*gegen*

"Versus" is used in sporting events (as well as in court cases) to show that
two people or teams are competing against each other.

<u>**What a**</u> **match!**	*Was für ein Spiel!*

1. Complete each sentence using the correct preposition.

1. Have you ever been _____ a placement?

2. He turned his attention _____ the letters on his desk.

3. What do you believe _____?

4. An increasing number of men are now _____ paternity leave.

5. Nowadays, we are completely dependent _____ computers.

6. _____ the end it all comes down to money.

7. She decided to take part _____ the race _____ the last minute.

2. Choose the correct word to complete each sentence.

1. Some people write down their appointments in a _____.
   a) calendar   b) diary

2. I missed my dentist's _____ last week.
   a) appointment   b) deadline

3. I should have finished the presentation last week – but I had so much to do that I missed the _____.
   a) appointment   b) deadline

4. I think I'll get a _____ with photographs of the desert to put on my wall next year.
   a) calendar   b) diary

3. **Find the phrasal verb which means the same as each expression below. Combine a verb from the left with a preposition from the right.**

to chill	at s.th.
to come	in for s.o.
to look	into s.o.
to run	into s.th.
to stand	out
to stick	s.o. over
to win	up with s.th.

a) to temporarily do s.o. else's job   _____

b) to persuade s.o. to agree with you _____

c) to keep on doing s.th.   _____

d) to relax and not do very much   _____

e) to think of s.th.   _____

f) to investigate s.th.   _____

g) to meet s.o. by chance   _____

Now complete these sentences using the appropriate phrasal verb.

1. I _____ Steve last week when I was at the

   library. He _____ Jane at the moment as
   she's off sick.

2. She _____ a great idea for a book and is now

   trying to _____ a publisher.

3. A lot of people are now starting to learn Chinese. However, quite

   a few don't _____ it and give up after a
   short while.

4. **Find the expressions to do with jobs which have the same meaning as the German ones. Combine a verb with a word or expression.**

> **to accept – to apply for – to be made – to be on – to go –**
>
> **to knock off – to quit**

> **freelance – a job – a job – a job offer – redundant –**
>
> **sick leave – work**

a) *eine Stelle annehmen* _____

b) *Feierabend machen* _____

c) *krankgeschrieben sein* _____

d) *kündigen* _____

e) *den Arbeitsplatz verlieren* _____

f) *freiberuflich tätig werden* _____

g) *sich für eine Stelle bewerben* _____

5. **Cross out the incorrect word or words in each of these sentences.**

1. Did you see the football (game / match) on TV last night? Manchester United won two (nil / love / zero).

2. If you want to stay healthy, it is very important to do (exercise / exercises).

3. The tennis (court / field / pitch) was badly damaged in the storm.

4. His parents have set up (funds / a fund) to pay for his education.

5. She's living on a state (pension / retirement).

6. **Complete the following idioms, then choose one to complete each of the sentences.**

| ears | eyes | neck | feet | feet |

a) to find one's _____

b) to breathe down s.o.'s _____

c) to be up to one's _____ / _____ in s.th.

d) to have itchy _____

1. I _____ work at the moment and my

   boss _____.

2. If you _____ and decide to go to live in

   a different country for a while, it might well take you some time

   to _____.

7. **Match the idioms on the left with their meanings on the right.**

1. to recharge one's batteries   a) to communicate regularly

2. in the middle of nowhere   b) the way a situation is developing

3. to cut a long story short   c) to rest in order to get your strength back

4. to keep in touch   d) to not give s.o. all the details but to be brief

5. to take the plunge   e) a place that is far away from other people

6. the lie of the land   f) to do s.th. difficult that you have thought about doing for a long time

Interview with the director

Last week our film **critic** sat down with Sam Stewart to talk about his **latest** film *Claude*. Here are a few excerpts:

Sam, in the past you directed a couple of action blockbusters and the major **box office hit** *Trapped.* *So what drew you towards a* **period drama** *this time?*
I'd been interested in exploring new genres for a while. When I read the **script**, I saw that it was a fascinating tale about art, about passion, about **breaking with tradition** and thought it was challenging material. **Funnily enough**, I hated a lot of period dramas and was a little surprised to then find myself directing one!

What made you **go for** *David in the* **lead role** *– did you always* **have him in mind***?*
Well, I just think he's an incredible actor – I absolutely loved his portrayal of Gareth in *Think Twice*. And I wasn't looking for anyone who **had a big name** – Dave's an **up-and-coming** actor who brings a certain freshness and newness to the role. When he **auditioned for** the part, my **gut feeling** just told me he'd be perfect.

The critics are **raving about** *his performance – do you think he might be nominated for an Oscar?*
He certainly deserves it! But we'll just have to **wait and see**.

Is it true that you also had a **cameo role** *in the film?*
(Laughs) I'm not **letting on** – you'll have to see the film again!!

Have you got any other films **in the pipeline***?*
Yes, I'm working on a fantasy film set in the future. We're making it **on location** in the Nevada desert. We've **come up with** a whole new language for the people and are going to **shoot it in** Sayspeak to make it more authentic and futuristic. Don't worry though, you won't have to learn it – there will be **subtitles**!

Which expression means the same as each of these phrasal verbs?	
1. to go for s.o. / s.th.	*a) to say s.th. that was meant to be secret*
2. to let on about s.th.	*b) to invent s.th.*
3. to come up with s.th.	*c) to choose s.o. / s.th.*

Talking about films	
box office hit	*Kassenschlager*
period drama	*Historiendrama*
script	*Drehbuch*
lead role	*Hauptrolle*
starring role	
cameo role	*Kurzauftritt*
to film / make s.th. on location	*einen Film vor Ort drehen*
to shoot s.th. in German	*etw. auf Deutsch drehen*
subtitles	*Untertitel*

"Surtitles" are what you see at an opera production when a translation of the text being sung appears above the stage.
If the voices on the soundtrack of a film are not those of the original actors but of other actors in a different language, we say the film has been "dubbed" *(synchronisiert)*.

to break with tradition	*mit einer Tradition brechen*
Note in English there is no article!	
funnily enough	*komischerweise, witzigerweise*
to have s.o. / s.th. in mind (for s.th.) *(idiom)*	*jdn. / etw. (für etw.) im Auge haben*
to bear s.th. in mind	*etw. berücksichtigen / nicht vergessen*
bearing in mind that …	*angesichts der Tatsache, dass …*
to have a big name	*eine Berühmtheit sein*
to have a good / bad name	*einen guten / schlechten Ruf haben*
up-and-coming *(idiom)*	*aufstrebend*
to audition [ɔːˈdɪʃn] **for s.th.**	*vorsprechen / -spielen für etw.*
to hold an audition	*jdn. vorsprechen / -spielen lassen*

The word "audition" is used for actors, singers, dancers and musicians.

gut feeling / instinct *(idiom)*	*Bauchgefühl*

Your "guts" are your internal organs, especially your intestines *(Darm)*. If someone says a person "has guts", it means he or she has courage. If you "hate someone's guts", then you really dislike the person. Both expressions are informal.

Wait and see! *(idiom)*	*Warten Sie es ab!*
to have s.th. in the pipeline *(idiom)*	*etw. in der Planung haben*
critic ❗	*Kritiker/in* p. 130

The translation of the German word *"neueste"* is "**latest**" or "most recent".

to rave about s.th.	*von etw. schwärmen*
Be careful: to rave against s.o. / s.th.	*gegen jdn. / etw. wettern*

NY Fashion Week – blog

Monday, 2 July

Fashion Week **kicked off** with Martini's ready-to-wear collection for spring-summer. The Italian designer impressed the audience with his simple and relaxed style, proving he is still able to set trends. In an interview afterwards he said he wanted to "go back to basics, because this is where it all began".

Saturday, 7 July

The week-long fashion extravaganza came to a dazzling close today. The Grand Palais was packed and the stars were out in force in the front rows to see Stark's new collection: Sophie Night went for a classic LBD, Sarah Parker had dressed down in jeans and a V-neck sweater and Jemma Davis was the height of fashion in a white blouse and this season's must-have black velvet jacket.

Stark unveiled a glittering collection perfect for A-listers looking for something extra special for the next awards season. It was all about exquisite details and luxury fabrics. And while many designers had used typical summer colours such as cream, lemon and light gray, Stark's catwalk was a riot of colour. One of the highlights was Lily Mason stepping out in a stunning red satin creation.

Comments

At least Martini's clothes won't go out of fashion so quickly.

I think Martini's clothes will be all the rage this summer! They're great for work but can be dressed up with accessories if you're going out at night, so you really **stand out**. I love them!

I wouldn't be seen dead in some of these clothes – only fashion victims would buy them!

Which expression means the same as each of these phrasal verbs?

1. to *kick off	a) to choose s.th.
2. to go for s.th.	b) to look different from others
3. to stand out	c) to start

Talking about fashion shows

ready-to-wear collection	*Konfektionskollektion*
off-the-peg *(BE, idiom)* off-the-rack *(AE, idiom)*	*Konfektions-, von der Stange*
off-the-peg suit	*Konfektionsanzug*
to unveil a collection to launch a collection	*eine Kollektion der Öffentlichkeit* *vorstellen*
catwalk runway (more common in *AE*)	*Laufsteg*

Talking about fashion

to dress down	*sich leger anziehen*

The expression "to give s.o. a dressing down" means to tell s.o. off *(jdm. eins auf den Deckel geben)*, e.g. "His boss gave him a dressing down for being late.".

to dress up	*sich fein anziehen*

If children "dress up" or "play dressing up", they put on special clothes and pretend to be different people *(sich verkleiden)*.

to dress s.th. up (with s.th.)	*etw. (mit etw.) verschönern*
to be the height of fashion	*hochmodisch sein*
to go out of fashion	*aus der Mode kommen*
to be all the rage *(inf.)*	*der letzte Schrei sein*
to not be seen dead in s.th. *(inf.)*	*etw. nie im Leben anziehen*
fashion victim *(humorous, idiom)*	*Modeopfer*
to set a (new) trend	*einen (neuen) Trend auslösen*
back to basics	*zurück zu den Wurzeln*
to come to a (dazzling) close	*ein (prachtvolles) Ende finden*
to be packed *(inf.)*	*brechend voll sein*
to be out in force *(idiom)*	*zahlreich erscheinen*
LBD (= little black dress)	*Kleine Schwarze*
must-have	*unbedingt nötig / „es geht nicht ohne"*

"Must-have" is mainly used as an adjective. The noun is usually "a must", e.g. "This dress is a must!" *(ein Muss)*.

A-lister = celebrity	*Promi*

The "A-list" refers to the most successful actors and actresses in Hollywood.
The "**awards season**" is usually used to talk about the time of year when different film prizes are awarded (e.g. Oscars, Golden Globes).

to be all about s.th. *(inf.)*	*sich um etw. drehen*
to be a riot of colour	*eine Farbenpracht sein*

"**Week-long**" means that something lasts for <u>one</u> week.

<u>front</u> row [rəʊ]	*erste Reihe*
fabric !	*Stoff*

p. 131

Online advertising

Presenter: Good evening and welcome to tonight's panel discussion on the **advertising industry**, the **Internet** and children. First of all, why are **advertising executives** so **interested in** reaching children?

Guest 1: Well, they're a very important **target group for several reasons**. They not only have their own **purchasing power**, but they also influence their parents' buying decisions – it's known as "**pester power**".

Guest 2: And don't forget, they're tomorrow's adult consumers. So companies are keen to **establish brand loyalty from an early age**.

Presenter: But there are **regulations on** advertising aimed at children. And there's an **advertising watchdog**, the Advertising Standards Authority, to make sure that these rules are not broken.

Guest 3: Absolutely, but the Internet has opened up new possibilities and it's very difficult to regulate what's going on there. Let me **give you an example**. A company might design their own website around a product, including games, competitions and even a community. The product is then part of the content of the website so **the lines become blurred** between advertising, entertainment and information.

Guest 1: It's also a way of collecting information about their customers – for instance by using online registration **forms**.

Guest 3: That's right, and they can use this information to **build up user profiles** of those who visit the site or even sell the information to **third parties.** Sometimes they use the website to **do market research** before they finally **launch a product**.

Guest 2: Another example is buzz marketing – a variant on the **tried and tested** "**by word of mouth**" method. The idea is to find the coolest kids and have them use or wear a product in order **to create a buzz about** it. And this is well-suited to the Internet, where so-called "Net promoters" **spread the word** about clothes, music and other products in newsgroups, chat rooms and blogs.

Guest 3: So **in other words, anything goes**.

Talking about advertising

advertising industry	*Werbebranche*

In English the word "industry" is used to refer to a particular branch of economic or commercial industry, e.g. "the tourist industry".

advertising executive [ɪgˈzekjətɪv]	*Werbemanager/in*

An "executive" is a senior manager in a company. The word can also be used as an adjective before a noun to mean having the power to make important decisions in an organization or government *(leitend)*, e.g. "She is an executive director at the bank.".

advertising watchdog	*Werberegulierungsbehörde*

A "watchdog" is a dog that is kept to look after a house or property. The word is also used figuratively to refer to a person or organization that monitors companies to make sure that they do not do anything illegal.

The word "**Internet**" can be written with a capital letter or a small letter.   p. 87

target group	*Zielgruppe*
purchasing power	*Kaufkraft*
pester power	*Aufzwingen seines Willens durch ständiges Nerven und Quengeln*
to establish brand loyalty	*Markenbindung aufbauen*
to blur the lines (between)	*die Grenzen verwischen (zwischen)*
to build up a user profile	*ein Benutzerprofil erstellen*
third party	*dritte Person*
to do market research	*Marktforschung betreiben*

You can also use the verbs "to carry out" or "to conduct" *(formal)*.

to launch [ɔː] **a product**	*ein Produkt auf den Markt bringen*

The verb "launch" is used to talk about sending missiles into the air, rockets into space as well as putting boats or ships into water. It can also be used in a figurative sense to talk about starting something, e.g. "to launch an investigation" *(eine Untersuchung starten)*, "to launch a campaign" *(eine Kampagne starten)*.

tried and tested *(idiom)*	*erprobt*
by word of mouth *(idiom)*	*mündlich*
to create a buzz (about s.th.) *(idiom)*	*einen Wirbel um etw. machen*
to spread the word *(inf., idiom)*	*es allen sagen*
anything goes *(idiom)*	*erlaubt ist, was gefällt*
to be interested <u>in</u> doing s.th.	*daran interessiert sein, etw. zu tun*
<u>for</u> several reasons	*aus mehreren Gründen*
from <u>an</u> early <u>age</u>	*von früh auf*
regulation <u>on</u> s.th.	*Vorschriften*
to <u>give</u> an example	*ein Beispiel nennen*
form !	*Formular* p. 131
<u>in</u> other words	*mit anderen Worten*

Where do you read the news?

❝ I prefer reading the news online. You **have access to** the news as it comes in. The print version is just not as **up-to-date** – if a story **breaks** after the newspaper has **gone to press**, you don't get to read it till the day after. ❞

❝ Well, online news sites often **give prominence to** stories that do not **hit the headlines** in newspapers as they are not really very important nationally or globally. But as there's so much competition amongst online news sites they are put at the top of the page to make people think they are really **up-to-the-minute**. ❞

❝ I'd rather read a printed newspaper because it offers more **in-depth coverage** and opinions. And I can read it on the train! ❞

❝ I think printed newspapers have a much better layout, especially the **front page**. Visual elements such as the placement of each story, its length and the headline help us to judge the importance of the **news item**. Some online newspapers just have a list of headlines, so global news stories **carry the same weight** as stories about celebrities. ❞

❝ I find online newspapers much more entertaining – you can watch live **news broadcasts** or interactive graphics, download podcasts, and get the **latest** information via RSS feeds. ❞

❝ It's **all the same to me** – it's all about **muck-raking** nowadays to get more readers. ❞

Another **near miss** in London

A bomb was found in central London early this morning. According to **eyewitness reports**, a blue Toyota crashed into rubbish bins on the pavement outside the Haymarket club at 5.30 a.m. The driver then jumped out and ran away. A **passer-by** immediately called the police, who cleared the area and carried out a controlled explosion.
The Prime Minister later **issued a statement** condemning the attempted bombing and promising a **full investigation**. [more …]

The "**silly season**" is a British term and usually refers to the time in the middle of summer when newspapers **run silly stories**, often **blowing them out of proportion** to fill their newspapers. It is generally when Parliament is **in recess**.

Talking about the press

to go to press	*in Druck gehen*
hot off the press	*druckfrisch*

In these two cases, the word "press" refers to the printing press (machine) used to print the newspaper.

to leak s.th. to the press	*etw. der Presse zuspielen*
to inform the press	

Here, "press" refers to the journalists working for newspapers. The word "press" also refers to newspapers and magazines, e.g. "the British press".

Talking about the news

to break (of news)	*ans Licht kommen, bekannt werden*
to hit the headlines	*Schlagzeilen machen*
in-depth coverage	*gründliche Berichterstattung*
to receive a lot of media coverage	*ein großes Medienecho erhalten*
<u>front</u> page (news)	*erste Seite, Titelseite*

"News" is uncountable. If only one piece of news is meant, then the expression used is "**a news item**" or "an item of news". p. 134

news broadcast	*Nachrichtensendung*
to run a story	*über etw. berichten*
to have access to s.th.	*hier: auf etw. zugreifen*
to give prominence to s.th.	*etw. in den Vordergrund stellen*
up-to-the-minute	*allerneuste, topaktuell*
to carry weight *(idiom)*	*Bedeutung haben*
it's all the same to me *(idiom)*	*das macht für mich keinen Unterschied*
muck-raking *(inf., idiom)*	*Sensationsjournalismus*
near miss *(idiom)*	*hier: eine knappe Sache*
eyewitness report	*Augenzeugenbericht*
to issue ['ɪʃuː] **a statement**	*eine Stellungnahme abgeben*
to issue a press release	*eine Pressemeldung herausgeben*
full investigation	*eine umfassende Untersuchung*
to conduct an investigation	*eine Untersuchung durchführen*
the silly season *(inf., idiom)*	*die Saure-Gurken-Zeit, das Sommerloch*
to blow s.th. out of proportion *(idiom)*	*etw. maßlos übertreiben*
to be in recess [rɪˈses]	*in der Sommerpause sein*

This expression is used to describe the holiday between periods of work in an official organization, court or parliament. In *AE* "recess" also refers to the break between lessons at school, i.e. what the British call "break".

The translation of the German word "*aktuell*" is **up-to-date**. ❗ p. 132
The translation of the German word "*neueste*" is "**latest**" or "most recent".
The plural of "**passer-by**" *(Passant/in)* is "passer<u>s</u>-by".

Cyber ethics ■ ■ ■ ■ ■ ■ ■ ■ ■ ■ ■ ■ ■ ■ ■ ■ ■

The **Internet** now touches most aspects of our personal, professional and social lives – we communicate **via the Internet**, we **surf the Net** for information, we shop **on the Internet** and we use it as a means of entertainment. The new digital age has **given rise to** a complex range of moral and ethical questions, **sparking controversy** and debate.

———————————

During our two-day seminar we will **explore the following issues** and analyse the **impact they will have on** the future of the Internet.

The right to remain anonymous

Anonymity has been a central aspect of the Internet **right from the start**. At the same time it is also a major obstacle to making it safe. Whether sending spam, distributing **offensive** and **illegal material**, or using it to organize terrorist activities, some people argue that these activities are all helped by the ease with which people can **mask their identity** in the online world. We will be examining the issues and weighing up **the pros and cons** of both sides.

Privacy

Many consumers now feel that they are being forced to **disclose too much personal information** on the Internet. Vast amounts of **data** are collected and stored. Companies **build up detailed profiles** of consumers, sometimes using the data in an unauthorized manner and selling it to third parties. Employers monitor the actions of their employees (for instance what **websites they are accessing** in company time) and governments monitor their citizens. To what extent are we now living in a post-privacy era?

Digital rights

The Internet has opened up a new debate about copyright and **intellectual property**. While the crime itself is not new, the PC and the Internet have facilitated the copying and distribution of material. Plagiarism and piracy **are rife** – people exchange and download games, music and other **content** without worrying that this is actually **prohibited**. Can this be regulated or do we have to accept that online content is free?

Phrasal verbs for computing

With the following phrasal verbs to do with computers, the object can go before the preposition or after it, e.g. "he backed his files up" or "he backed up his files":
to filter out (spam); **to back up** (a file); **to type in / to key in** (a password / an address); **to print out** (a document)
But remember, when writing it is better not to end the sentence with a preposition, e.g. "He printed out the letter." not "He printed the letter out.".

Talking about the Internet

The word "**Internet**" can be written with a capital letter or a small letter. The same is true of the abbreviation "Net" or "net".

<u>via</u> / over **the Internet**	*übers Internet*
to surf the Net	*im Netz surfen*
<u>on</u> **the Internet**	*im Internet*
to be / go <u>on</u> the Internet	*im Internet sein / ins Internet gehen*
to be connected <u>to</u> the Internet	*mit dem Internet verbunden sein*
to access a website	*eine Website aufrufen*

Talking about forbidding something

There are different ways of saying that something is not allowed in English. On signs you might simply see "No photographs". Other possibilities are:

… is (strictly) prohibited   *… ist (strengstens) verboten / untersagt*

This expression formally forbids something, usually by law or some other authority. It is seen on official signs, e.g. "Smoking prohibited".

it is (strictly) forbidden to do s.th.   *es ist (strengstens) verboten, etw. zu tun*

You are not allowed to …   *Man darf etw. nicht …*

… is not allowed   *… ist nicht erlaubt*

The German construction "*es ist nicht erlaubt*" cannot be translated word for word – use one of the above phrases. "… not allowed" is the least formal.

to give rise to a question	*eine Frage aufwerfen*
to spark controversy [ˈkɒntrəvɜːsɪ]	*Kontroversen entfachen*

The following verbs can also be used instead of "to spark": "to create", "to stir" or "to fuel". In all cases there is no article in front of "controversy".

to explore an issue [ˈɪʃuː] / **a question** *eine Frage untersuchen*

to have an impact [ˈɪmpækt] **on s.th.** *Auswirkungen auf etw. haben*

The verb "to make" can also be used. Note, the noun is in the singular!

(right) from the start	*von Anfang an*	
offensive material	*anstößige Inhalte*	
to mask one's identity	*seine Identität verbergen*	
the pros and cons *(idiom)*	*die Vor- und Nachteile*	p. 158
to disclose information	*Informationen preisgeben*	
to build up a profile of s.o.	*ein Profil von jdm. erstellen*	
intellectual property	*geistiges Eigentum*	
to be rife [raɪf]	*weit verbreitet sein*	

The opposite of "legal" is "**<u>il</u>legal**". The prefix "il-" is also used to form the opposite of the adjectives "legible" *(lesbar)*, "logical" *(logisch)* and "literate" *(beschreibt jemand, der Lesen und Schreiben kann)*.

The noun "**data**" *(Daten)* is uncountable and is followed by a singular or plural verb, e.g. "The data is / are on my PC.". It is treated as a plural noun (singular "datum") in scientific writing, e.g. "These data must be checked.".

content   *Inhalt*   p. 110

1. **Complete each of these sentences using the correct preposition.**

1. The film was originally shot _____ Japanese.

2. The critics are raving _____ his new book – they say it's the best one he's ever written.

3. I read about the film _____ the Internet.

4. She's always been interested _____ doing a placement abroad.

5. We need stricter regulations _____ product placement in films _____ several reasons.

6. How many computers are connected _____ the Internet?

7. Does she have the right skills for this musical? _____ other words, can she sing and dance as well as act?

2. **Choose the correct phrasal verb to complete each of these sentences.**

> **to come up with s.th. – to go for s.th. – to kick off –
> to let on – to stand out**

1. They asked a PR agency to _____ their new online campaign. –

   Which agency did they _____?

2. _____ in this turquoise jacket this winter!

3. What time does the meeting _____ today?

4. Yesterday, Susan _____ that she is up for promotion next month.

3. The words on the right have been jumbled up. Work each one out, then combine one of the words on the right with one on the left to find expressions relating to the press.

front	potrer	_____
eyewitness	egaveroc	_____
news	teamstent	_____
media	gape	_____
to issue a	dacatrobs	_____
news	miet	_____

4. Find the expressions which have the same meaning as the German ones. Combine a verb with a word or expression from the boxes below to find the expressions relating to advertising and the Internet.

> to access – to build up – to create – to disclose –
> to do – to launch

> a buzz – information – market research – a product –
> a profile – a website

a) *eine Website aufrufen*   _____

b) *Marktforschung betreiben*   _____

c) *ein Profil erstellen*   _____

d) *ein Produkt auf den Markt
   bringen*   _____

e) *einen Wirbel machen*   _____

f) *Informationen preisgeben*   _____

5. **Complete the following sentences to do with films.**

1. If a film is not shown in the original but has been translated into another language, it has been _____.

2. If someone only has a very small role in a film, they have a _____, the main actor is in the _____.

3. The person who writes a review of a film is called a _____.

4. Some films are made in studios, others are filmed _____.

6. **Which expression or word is the odd one out in each case?**

1. ❏ factory   ❏ fabric   ❏ material

2. ❏ to have guts   ❏ to have courage   ❏ to have stomach ache

3. ❏ to spark controversy ❏ to stir controversy ❏ to avert controversy

4. ❏ to wear casual clothes ❏ to wear formal clothes ❏ to dress down

5. ❏ to be full   ❏ to be empty   ❏ to be packed

6. ❏ to dress s.o. down   ❏ to tell s.o. off   ❏ to change s.o.'s clothes

7. ❏ to be widespread   ❏ to be ready   ❏ to be rife

8. ❏ to bear s.th. in mind ❏ to consider s.th.   ❏ to forget s.th.

7. Match the idioms on the left with their meanings on the right.

1. the pros and cons	a) to tell people about s.th.
2. tried and tested	b) to be planning s.th. that will happen in the future
3. the silly season	c) used by many people and proven to be true
4. to spread the word	d) reasons for and against
5. gut feeling	e) to be important and have influence
6. to carry weight	f) a person who buys too many fashionable clothes
7. fashion victim	g) a feeling that you think must be right
8. to have s.th. in the pipeline	h) period of time in the summer when there is not very much news

Now put the correct idiom into each of these sentences.

1. His opinion always _____ with the boss.

2. Their new laptop is due to be launched in the spring. My _____ tells me it's going to be a real hit.

3. A _____ way of curing hiccoughs is to eat sugar.

4. She always buys the latest clothes, even if they don't suit her – she's a real _____!

5. Have you considered all _____ ?

6. By the way, can you _____ that we're now meeting after lunch tomorrow?

Talking about books

"This collection of anecdotes and quotations by Oscar Wilde **makes perfect bedtime reading** as you can **dip into** it **at will**. It's also **highly entertaining**."

"I read John Grisham's *The Firm* from **cover to cover** in **one sitting**. It's been called a **compulsive read** and I certainly **couldn't put it down**. It's full of action and twists and keeps **catching the reader by surprise**."

"Ondaatje's *The English Patient* is one of the most **extremely moving** books I've ever read. **It's set in** Italy at the end of World War II and **tells the story of** how four characters come together whose lives have been changed by their experiences. The story is **spellbinding** and is also **beautifully written**."

"To be honest, I found it rather difficult to **get into** Dickens' *Bleak House*. At times it was quite **heavy-going** and I **ended up skimming through** some of the longer descriptive passages. The plot is very complex and **difficult to follow**. You need **a lot of time on your hands** to read this."

"I just love Austen's *Pride and Prejudice*. For me its **lasting appeal lies in** the way Austen gently **pokes fun at** her characters and their pretensions. At the same time her characters are unforgettable and most readers will identify with the heroine, Elizabeth Bennett. It's a classic!"

"*To kill a Mockingbird* is one of my **all-time favourites**. The story is **presented through the eyes of** a child, which means it has an innocent and **down-to-earth** quality despite the fact that it **deals with** weighty **issues** like justice and prejudice. Harper Lee's characters are unforgettable!"

Which expression means the same as each of these phrasal verbs?

1. to dip into s.th.	a) to start enjoying s.th.
2. to get into s.th.	b) to finally do s.th.
3. to end up (doing s.th.)	c) to read small parts of s.th.

Talking about what books are like

highly entertaining	*sehr unterhaltsam*
extremely moving	*sehr ergreifend*
spellbinding / gripping	*fesselnd*
challenging	*anspruchsvoll*
shallow	*oberflächlich*
beautifully written	*schön geschrieben*
heavy-going	*mühsam*
thought-provoking	*nachdenklich stimmend*

"Very" is often overused in English. To make your writing more interesting, use intensifying adverbs such as "highly", "extremely", "incredibly". However, do be careful because some words can only be combined with specific adverbs, e.g. "highly entertaining" but "extremely/ incredibly moving".

p. 186

to make perfect bedtime reading	*die perfekte Bettlektüre sein*
at will	*beliebig*
to read s.th. from cover to cover	*(ein Buch) von Anfang bis zum Ende lesen*
in one sitting *(idiom)*	*auf einmal*

You can also say "at one sitting".

to be a compulsive read	*man muss es einfach lesen*
to be compulsive reading	
to be a good read	*sich gut lesen lassen*
to not be able to put s.th. down	*etw. nicht aus der Hand legen können*
to catch s.o. by surprise	*jdn. überraschen*
to take s.o. by surprise	
to be set in	*spielen in*
to tell the story of	*die Geschichte erzählen von*
to skim through a book	*ein Buch überfliegen*
difficult to follow	*schwer zu folgen*
to have (a lot of) time on one's hands *(idiom)*	*(viel) Zeit zur Verfügung haben*
its lasting appeal lies in	*sein anhaltender Reiz besteht darin*
to have lasting appeal	*einen anhaltenden Reiz ausüben*
all-time favourite	*absoluter Lieblings-*
down-to-earth *(idiom)*	*bodenständig*
to deal with an issue ['ɪʃuː]	*sich mit einem Thema befassen*
to poke fun at s.o. *(idiom)*	*sich über jdn. lustig machen*
to make fun of s.o.	
to present s.th. through s.o.'s eyes	*etw. aus jds. Perspektive erzählen*

Art at auction

Wednesday, 16 May 2007

Sotheby's Spring Evening Sale of Contemporary Art made auction history yesterday. Mark Rothko's *White Center (Yellow, Pink and Lavender on Rose)*, dating from 1950, sold for the record price of $72,800,000. This set a new record for a contemporary, post-war work of art at auction and exceeded everyone's expectations. It came from the collection of David Rockefeller and went to an anonymous buyer.

Another highlight of the sale was Francis Bacon's striking masterpiece *Study from Innocent X*. It went for $52,680,000 – a record for the artist to date. In total, 74 works by artists as diverse as Andy Warhol, Jean-Michel Basquiat, Roy Lichtenstein and Willem de Kooning to name but a few, were up for auction. At the end of the sale all but nine of them had been snapped up. The evening brought in a total of $254,874,000.

Comments

Words fail me – how can someone pay money for a painting that any six-year-old can do?!

Talk about paying through the nose!

Rothko has finally hit the big time! Cool – he's a great artist!

Which expression means the same as each of these phrasal verbs?

1) to go to s.o.	*a) to be sold for*
2) to go for	*b) to make (money)*
3) to snap s.th. up	*c) to be acquired by s.o.*
4) to bring in (money)	*d) to buy s.th. because you think it is a bargain or just what you want*

Talking about art and the arts

"**Art**" also "fine art" is used to refer to paintings, drawings and sculptures, e.g. "Art is his best subject at school.". It can also refer to technique and creativity, e.g. "She is studying the art of photography.".
The term "the arts" refers to all of the different branches of creative activity such as painting, music, film, literature and dance. It is a plural noun.
The "performing arts" refers to dance, opera, music, the theatre and film.
"The arts" is also used to refer to subjects that are not scientific or technical, such as languages, history and literature *(Geisteswissenschaften)*, e.g. "an arts graduate", "to do an arts degree".

work of art	*Kunstwerk*
arts page	*Feuilleton*

If someone is "artistic", they have natural creative talent *(kreativ)*, e.g. "I'm not very artistic.".
"Artistic" also means relating to art or artists *(künstlerisch)*, e.g. "The censors wanted to abolish artistic freedom.".
If a design or arrangement is "artistic", then it means it is aesthetically pleasing *(kunstvoll)*, e.g. "an artistic arrangement of flowers".

artistic talent / ability	*künstlerische Begabung*
artistic director	*künstlerische/r Leiter/in*

Talking about paintings

A painting or sculpture might be	**striking** sophisticated intriguing tongue-in-cheek *(idiom)* run-of-the-mill *(idiom)*	*auffallend anspruchsvoll faszinierend ironisch durchschnittlich*

at auction [ˈɔːkʃn]	*zur Versteigerung (kommen)*
to make history	*Geschichte schreiben*
to date from	*stammen von / aus dem Jahr*
to set a record [ˈrekɔːd]	*einen Rekord aufstellen*
to exceed s.o.'s expectations	*jds. Erwartungen übertreffen*
to live up to s.o.'s expectations	*jds. Erwartungen erfüllen*
to date	*bis heute*
to name but a few	*unter anderem*
to be up for auction	*zur Versteigerung angeboten werden*
words fail me *(idiom)*	*mir fehlen die Worte*
talk about … *(inf.)*	*hier: so was von …*
to pay through the nose *(idiom)*	*einen Wucherpreis bezahlen*
to hit the big time *(idiom)*	*seinen Durchbruch feiern*

Remember, in English the currency symbol comes <u>before</u> the amount and there is no gap between the symbol and the first number. Unlike in German, a decimal point is used, e.g. £4.50. Large numbers can be made more readable using commas, e.g. **$72,800,000**. p. 178

European tour – blog

XxX finally arrived in Dresden last night **to kick off** the **final leg of** their European tour **to promote their latest album**. The venue was sold out – some fans had **forked out** hundreds of euros to see them live. After a short opening act, everyone waited for over half an hour for *XxX* to **make their entrance**. And then they finally appeared, rising from under the stage on a mechanical platform. They opened with the hit single "Screaming" which **shot to number one** three months ago. Immediately the crowd started **singing along** with this **catchy tune**, in fact a lot of people seemed to know the **lyrics** to all the songs. Visually, the show was spectacular. **No expense was spared** with dazzling light shows, fireworks, smoke, flames and lasers.
It was a truly unforgettable experience.

Classical music – a nineteenth century superstar

Hello and welcome to 'Famous Musicians'. Today we've invited the musicologist Stephen Rower to talk about Nicolò Paganini.

When did Paganini start playing the violin?

Not that early, actually. He was seven when he **took it up** and thirteen when he **gave his first public performance** in 1793.

Paganini has been called the first superstar. Why?

Well, **first and foremost** he was a **virtuoso on** the violin and one of the greatest violinists to ever have lived. He **had an extremely good ear** – he always **played in tune** – and was extremely innovative. It was this technical ability, his showmanship and his wild, romantic appearance that made him a **roaring success** with the **public**.

How did people in his day react towards him?

Very much as they do towards superstars nowadays! Ladies in the **audience** sometimes fainted when he played, for instance. He **had a huge following** and was often **mobbed by fans**.

What pieces did he play?

He performed his own works, which were incredibly difficult, mostly playing **from memory**.

Talking about playing an instrument

to take up an instrument	*anfangen ein Instrument zu spielen*
to play an instrument	*ein Instrument spielen*
to tune an instrument	*ein Instrument stimmen*

Remember in English you need an article when you talk about playing or learning an instrument, e.g. "I play <u>the</u> piano.".

to be a virtuoso on an instrument	*ein Virtuose/eine Virtuosin auf einem Instrument sein*
virtuoso pianist	*begnadete/r Pianist/in*
to have a good ear (for s.th.) *(idiom)*	*ein gutes Gehör haben*
to play by ear	*nach dem Gehör spielen*
to play in / out of tune	*richtig / falsch spielen*

If you are "in tune with s.o. / s.th.", you are in agreement with the person or you sympathize with him or her, e.g. "She was in tune with nature." *(in Einklang mit etw. / jdm. sein)*. The opposite is "out of tune with s.o. / s.th.".

The idiom "to change your tune" means you change your opinion, e.g. "He changed his tune after the accident." *(die Meinung ändern)*.

to play from memory	*auswendig spielen*
to kick s.th. off *(inf.)*	*etw. starten*
first / final leg of s.th.	*erster / letzter Abschnitt einer Sache*
to promote an album	*für ein Album Werbung machen*
to release an album	*ein Album veröffentlichen*
to fork out money for s.th. *(inf.)*	*für etw. Geld locker machen*
to make an entrance	*in Erscheinung treten, auftreten*
to shoot to number one	*sofort an die Spitze der Charts gelangen*
catchy tune	*Ohrwurm*
no expense (was) spared *(idiom)*	*Kosten spielten keine Rolle*
classical music	*klassische Musik*	p. 110
to give a performance	*auftreten*
first and foremost *(idiom)*	*zu allererst*
to be a roaring success *(idiom)*	*ein Bombenerfolg sein*
to have a huge following	*sehr viele Anhänger haben*

"To be mobbed by fans" has nothing to do with the German meaning of the word "*mobben*", it means being surrounded *(von Fans umringt werden)*.

to sing <u>along</u> (<u>with</u> s.o. / s.th.)	*mitsingen bei jdm. / etw.*
lyrics	*Liedtext*

The German word "*Text*" has different translations in English. We talk about the "lines" in a play, the "lyrics" in a song and the "script" of a speech.

public !	*öffentlich*	p. 131
the public	*die Öffentlichkeit*
<u>in</u> s.o.'s day	*zu jds. Zeit*
audience	*Publikum*	p. 120

Singers wanted!

Interested in **auditioning for** our new production of *Chicago*? If you think **you have what it takes**, book an audition!

Auditions are **by appointment only**. Please call 519 1761 1112 on September 14th, 15th, 23rd, or 24th between 8 p.m. and 10 p.m.

PREPARATION: Auditioners **are required to** bring a non-returnable photo. They should arrive fifteen minutes early to fill out an audition **form** and **be prepared to** stay about an hour. Singers should prepare one medium tempo song, preferably something jazzy, from any musical except *Chicago*.

Rave reviews

The Importance of Being There!
By Julie Fisher

The **opening night** of Wilde's *The Importance of Being Earnest* at the Theatre Royal was an absolute delight.

Tom Martin's set is simple yet elegant, allowing the **audience** to focus fully on Wilde's witty dialogue and message. And this message – what seems serious is often trivial, and **vice versa** – still **holds true** today.

The cast, made up of **up-and-coming** young actors and actresses, certainly **does the play justice**. They **deliver** the well-known **lines** with freshness and originality. David Green **hits the right note** with Algernon, playing him as Oscar Wilde himself. Ian Shaw is excellent as the long-suffering Jack Worthing and Jane Farmer **carries off the role** of Gwendolen Fairfax with just the right amount of superiority. Kevin Wear, a **natural comic**, **gives a memorable performance** as Lane, Algernon's straight-laced butler.

But it is Sarah George as the formidable Lady Bracknell who **steals the show**. Her **comic timing** is perfect and her delivery of lines such as "To lose one parent, Mr. Worthing, may be regarded as a misfortune; to lose both looks like carelessness." leaves the audience **roaring with laughter**.

An excellent evening's entertainment!

Theatre Royal, 16 May to 25 June
Running time: two-and-a-half hours with one **interval**

Talking about laughing

to giggle	*kichern*
to chuckle	*in sich hineinlachen*
to roar <u>with</u> laughter	*vor Lachen brüllen*
to howl with laughter *(inf.)*	*sich krummlachen*
to laugh one's head off *(idiom)*	*sich totlachen*

to audition [ɔːˈdɪʃn] for s.th.	*vorsprechen / -spielen für etw.*
to hold an audition	*jd. vorsprechen / -spielen lassen*

The word "audition" is used for singers, actors, dancers and musicians.

to have what it takes (to do s.th.)	*das Zeug dazu haben, etw. zu tun*
to be required to do s.th.	*etw. tun müssen*
to be prepared to do s.th.	*bereit sein, etw. zu tun*
opening night / premiere	*Premiere*

It is more usual to talk about the "opening night" of a play and the "premiere" of an opera.

vice versa	*(und) umgekehrt*
to hold true	*zutreffen*
up-and-coming *(idiom)*	*aufstrebend*
to do s.th. justice (to s.th.)	*etw. gerecht werden*
to deliver one's lines	*seinen Text vortragen*
to learn one's lines	*seinen Text lernen*

Be careful: The words of an actor's part are referred to as "lines".

to hit the right note *(idiom)*	*den richtigen Ton treffen*
to hit the wrong note *(idiom)*	*den falschen Ton treffen*
to carry off a role *(idiom)*	*in einer Rolle überzeugen*
natural comic	*von Natur aus ein/e Komödiant/in*
to give a memorable performance	*eine beeindruckende Vorstellung geben*
to steal the show *(idiom)*	*(den anderen) die Schau stehlen*
comic timing	*perfektes Timing beim Vortragen der Pointe*

<u>by</u> appointment only	*nur nach Vereinbarung*	p. 118
form !	*Formular*	

The translation of the German word "*Kritik*" is "**review**". **!** p. 132

a rave review	*eine glänzende Kritik / eine „Bombenkritik"*
bad / good / favourable review	*schlechte / gute / positive Rezension*

Be careful: if a play "bombs", it means it is a flop or failure.

audience	*Publikum*	p. 120

The break in a play, concert or film is called an "**interval**" or in *AE* "intermission". The gap between lessons at school or in a meeting is called a "break". The word "pause" is only used for a break in a conversation, e.g. "There was a short pause before Sarah said anything.". p. 122

1. **Choose the correct preposition to complete each of these sentences. Each preposition may only be used once.**

> along – at – by – from – in – out of – through – with

1. The story is presented _____ the eyes of the narrator.

2. In his latest work, the author pokes fun _____ our materialistic culture.

3. Auditions are _____ appointment only.

4. _____ Dickens' day, people often read novels in monthly instalments.

5. I can't sing _____, I don't know the words to this song.

6. The violin is a difficult instrument to learn because it often sounds _____ tune.

7. The audience roared _____ laughter at his jokes.

8. Can your recite any poems _____ memory?

2. **Underline the correct word in each of these sentences.**

1. This film is over three hours so there is (an interval / a pause) in the middle.

2. Pupils may not leave the school premises at (break / pause).

3. When the interviewer asked about his personal life, there was a short (break / pause / intermission) before he answered.

4. Smoking is not allowed in the theatre during the (break / interval).

3. **Choose the correct phrasal verb to complete each of these sentences. Use the verb in the right tense.**

> to bring in – to dip into – to get into – to go to –
> to snap up

1. The band auctioned off a signed guitar for charity – it

   _____ over £20,000.

2. She went to an art gallery last week and _____
   several works by a young Scottish artist.

3. Several of Jane Austen's letters were auctioned last week – they

   _____ an anonymous buyer.

4. I _____ *Great Expectations* on several

   occasions but I can never really _____ it.

4. **The words below have been jumbled up and all have to do with books. What are they?**

whalsol

_____

gnovmi

_____

vaehy-ignog

_____

gingpirp

book

_____

billdingpens

_____

tguhoth-korvongip

_____

itangrentine

_____

5. Combine these verbs with the nouns below. Then translate them into German.

to give	to hold	to make	to make
to release	to steal	to take up	

1. _____ history _____

2. _____ a performance _____

3. _____ an album _____

4. _____ an instrument _____

5. _____ the show _____

6. _____ an audition _____

7. _____ an entrance _____

6. "Art" or "arts"? Read the following sentences and decide which answer is the correct one in each case.

1. She wants to be a graphic designer and is going to _____ college next year.

2. There's an interesting review of the play on the _____ page today.

3. She has a very impressive _____ collection.

4. She's going to do an _____ degree – probably history.

5. Are you interested in modern _____? – Not really, I

   have to admit, I prefer the performing _____.

7. **Choose the correct idiom to replace the underlined expression in each of these sentences. Don't forget to make sure that it is grammatically correct!**

> to be a roaring success   to change one's tune
> to hit the right note   no expense was spared
> to poke fun at   to steal the show   up-and-coming

1. How much did the gallery spend on the Picasso? – I don't know exactly, but <u>they were obviously prepared to spend as much as necessary</u> _____.

2. He used not to really care about politics but he <u>changed his mind</u> _____ after he started helping the homeless.

3. The lead actor was brilliant – but it was the actress playing the maid who <u>was the best</u> _____.
Apparently, she's <u>considered to be a very promising</u>
_____ actress.

4. The critic's comments <u>were very true</u>
_____ – we thoroughly agreed with him.

5. The playwright <u>is making fun of</u> _____ the government in his latest play – <u>the audience has loved it</u>
_____ on Broadway.

Easily confused words

Homophones

Homophones are words with different meanings that are spelt differently but pronounced the same way. This can be confusing – even for native speakers – and often leads to spelling mistakes.

> Look at the words "**past**" and "**passed**". They sound the same but mean different things. Which word fits which sentence?
>
> The car drove _____ very fast.
>
> I've just _____ my driving test.

Accents may affect whether words are homophones or not. For instance in the US, "**due**" and "**do**" are pronounced alike, but they sound different if spoken by a British person. So always listen to the context – this will help you to understand the meaning.

Unfortunately there are no rules to help you to remember the differences between the words – you will just have to learn them. Some of them will be very familiar – such as "**to**", "**two**" and "**too**", "**there**", "**their**" and "**they're**", etc. Here are some other common ones which you should learn if you do not already know them.

['ɔːltə]
The church has a very old **altar**. *(Altar)*
Did you remember to **alter** our address? *(verändern)*

[ɔː]
They gazed in **awe** at the Crown Jewels. *(Ehrfurcht)*
An **oar** is a pole with a flat blade which is used to row a boat. *(Ruder)*
Iron **ore** is a rock **or** mineral from which iron is extracted. *(Erz)*, *(oder)*

['brɪtn]
A **Briton** is a native of **Britain**. *(Brite / Britin)*, *(Großbritannien)*

[tʃek]
Could you **check** whether the **cheque** has arrived? *(prüfen)*, *(Scheck)*
NB The word "cheque" is spelt "check" in AE.

[kɔːs]
The dog's hair is really **coarse**. *(rauh, grob)*
What **course** are you taking this year? *(Kurs)*
We're having a three-**course** meal. *(Gang)*
This event changed the **course** of history. *(Lauf)*

Here are some familiar homophones which even British people get wrong. Look at the sentences. Each one contains a pair (or sometimes a set of three) homophones. Decide which set is correct and then put each of the words into the right gap.

ate – eight	board – bored	brake – break
heal – heel	knew – new	paw – poor
tail – tale	their – there – they're	to – too – two
weather – whether		

1. We were not sure _____ the _____

   was going to improve over the weekend.

2. Would you _____ like to come _____

   the cinema, _____?

3. That _____ dog has hurt its _____.

4. Do you think _____ going to build _____ new

   headquarters over _____?

5. She _____ that he was _____ to the area.

6. This _____ is about a dog with a magic _____.

7. They were hungry and each of them _____

   _____ sausages!

8. He doesn't always _____ in time when he's on his

   bike – one day he'll fall off and _____ his arm.

9. Even if you're _____, you can still look at the

   _____!

10. The doctor said his _____ will _____

    quickly.

['kʌrənt]
Do you like **currant** cake? *(Rosine, also Johannisbeer)*
I started my **current** job last winter. *(aktuell)*
The **current** is very strong here along the coast. *(Strömung, Strom)*

[drɑːft]
Would you look through the first **draft** of my speech? *(Entwurf)*
Please close the window, there's a **draught**. *(Luftzug)*
NB The word "draught" is often spelt "draft" in AE.

[feə]
The decision was very **fair**. *(gerecht, also blond, hell, schön)*
Are you going to the **fair**? *(Messe, Kirmes)*
What's the return **fare** to London? *(Fahrpreis)*

['fɔːməlɪ]
He was **formally** introduced to her parents. *(förmlich, also formal)*
The art gallery was **formerly** housed in a factory. *(früher)*

['maɪnə]
Miners work in mines. *(Bergarbeiter/in)*
It is illegal to sell alcohol to **minors**. *(minderjährige Person)*
He made a **minor** mistake. *(gering, unbedeutend, also Moll)*

[preɪ]
They all **prayed** for peace. *(beten)*
Tigers use their large teeth to grab and kill **prey**. *(Beute, also ausbeuten, plündern)*

['prɪnsəpl]
Our **principal** aim is to raise money. *(Haupt-, wichtigste)*
The **principal** of a school is the head teacher. *(Rektor/in, Chef/in)*
Our party believes in the **principle** of free education. *(Prinzip, also Grundsatz)*

[saɪt]
The ancient **site** was a very impressive **sight**. *(Sehenswürdigkeit, also Lage, Bauplatz), (Anblick, also Sicht)*

BE [steɪʃnrɪ], *AE* [steɪʃnerɪ],
The car was **stationary**. *(stehend)*
The company has new **stationery**. *(Briefpapier, also Schreibwaren)*

[stɔːrɪ]
This building has six **storeys**. *(Etage, Stockwerk)*
His dad is reading him a **story**. *(Geschichte)*
NB The word "storey" is usually spelt "story" in AE.

Choose the correct word in each of these sentences. Use the verbs in the right tense.

1. Are you going to watch the _____ (currant / current) affairs programme tonight?

2. Sri Lanka, _____ (formally / formerly) known as Ceylon, is an island in the Indian Ocean.

3. I agree with you in _____ (principal / principle).

4. Alcohol must not be sold to _____ (miners / minors).

5. Is this the _____ (sight / site) for the new school?

6. My new boss is sending me a _____ (draft / draught) of the contract next week.

7. People's attitude _____ (altar / alter) if they have children.

8. Everyone _____ (pray / prey) for the safe release of the hostages this time last year.

9. The _____ (coarse / course) material can be downloaded from the university website.

10. The coach collided with a _____ (stationary / stationery) vehicle.

11. The orchestra is playing Beethoven's Ninth Symphony in D _____ (miner / minor).

Similar words

There are other words that are often easily confused – either because they look or sound similar. Here is a list with some of them, as well as information on their usage.

advice – advise

The noun "**advice**" *(Ratschlag, Rat)* is written with a "c" and pronounced [əd'vaɪs]. Remember it is uncountable – so you give someone "**a piece of** or **some advice**". You also get or give **advice on** or **about** s.th.

The verb "**to advise**" *(raten)* is written with an "s" and pronounced [əd'vaɪz].

You **advise s.o. on** or **about** s.th.

You **advise s.o. to do** s.th. or you **advise doing** s.th. if no person is mentioned, e.g. "She **advised me to go** to the doctor." but "She **advised going** by bus rather than by train.".

affect – effect

"**To affect**" is a verb and means to influence something *(beinflussen)*. An "**effect**" is the result or consequence of an action or process *(Wirkung)*. Look at how both words can be used in this sentence, "The law does not **affect** me / does not **have an effect** on me.".

And remember, the noun "effect" forms part of words such as "side effects" *(Nebenwirkungen)*, "special effects" and "greenhouse effect" *(Treibhauseffekt)*.

all together – altogether

"**All together**" means everyone *(alle zusammen)*, e.g. "When was the last time we were **all together**?".

The word "**altogether**" means completely *(insgesamt, völlig, ganz)*, "I stopped seeing him **altogether**.". If used after a number or a sum of money, it means in total, e.g. "That's £25.99 **altogether**, please.".

antique – antiquity

An "**antique**" is something that is very old and valuable *(Antiquität)*, e.g. "They have started collecting **antiques**.". It can also be used as an adjective to mean old, e.g. "She loves **antique** furniture." *(antik)*. "**Antiquity**" *(Antike)* refers to the ancient past, e.g. "These vases date from classical **antiquity**.".

Read the following sentences and decide which answer is the correct one in each case.

1. Can you give me _____?

   a) advise   b) some advice   c) an advice

2. _____ is another word for ancient times.

   a) antiquity   b) antiques   c) antique

3. When are we going to be _____ again?

   a) all together   b) altogether

4. She _____ the PM on foreign policy issues.

   a) some advice   b) advices   c) advises

5. I love looking around _____ shops, don't you?

   a) antiquity   b) antique   c) antiques

6. The special _____ were incredible.

   a) effect   b) affects   c) effects

7. _____ I'm happy it's now all over.

   a) all together   b) altogether

8. The film _____ her deeply.

   a) effected   b) affected

"Listen, when the side effects of this medication kick in, you'll forget what was wrong in the first place!"

beside – besides

"Beside" is a preposition and means "next to", e.g. "He put the book down beside me.".

"Besides" means "in addition to" or "apart from" *(außer, zusätzlich)*, e.g. "Is anyone else going to the party besides us?".

If "besides" is followed by a verb, it is in the -ing form, e.g. "Besides playing the violin, she also plays the flute.".

classic – classical – Classics

"Classic" can be used as an adjective *(klassisch)* and a noun *(Klassiker)*. Look at these two examples:

"This is a classic example of bad design."

"Have you read War and Peace – it's a classic!"

If you read "Classics" at university, you study Greek and Latin literature, philosophy and history.

The adjective "classical" is used in connection with music, "I prefer classical music to jazz." *(klassische Musik)* and with things belonging to the antiquity, e.g. "Are you interested in classical mythology?".

content – contents

"Content" is both an adjective and a noun. The adjective is pronounced [kən'tent] and means "happy" *(zufrieden)*. It cannot be used in front of a noun but only after verbs such as "feel", "look", "seem", "be" or "sound", e.g. "She looks really content.".

If "content" is used as a noun, it is pronounced ['kɒntent] and means "subject", "meaning" or "story" or "the amount of a particular substance in something" *(gedanklicher Inhalt, enthaltener Anteil / Gehalt)*. Look at these examples:

"What is the sugar content of this cereal?"

"The play lacked content."

The word "contents" means "the things that are inside something" *(alles, was enthalten ist)*, e.g. "He picked up the cup and drank the contents.". It also refers to the "table of contents" in a book *(Inhaltsverzeichnis)*.

dependant – dependent

A "dependant" *(Abhängige/r)* is someone who is financially "dependent" *(abhängig)* on someone else, usually a family member. However, the noun is increasingly being spelt the same way as the adjective. Remember, you are "dependent on" someone.

Put the correct word in each sentence. Each word may only be used once. And if the word needs to be in the plural, don't forget to do this.

beside	besides	besides	classic
classic	classical	Classics	content
content	contents	dependant	dependent

1. They put up the _____ of their house for auction.

2. Are you going to read _____ at university?

3. How many _____ does he have? –

   Well, _____ Jenny, he also has two children from a previous relationship.

4. I love going to _____ concerts, don't you?

5. Come over here and stand _____ me – you'll be able to see better.

6. You shouldn't be so _____ on what other people think.

7. The _____ of the film is not suitable for children.

8. This black dress is a real _____ – it won't go out of fashion.

9. Ever since she moved to Italy, she's been really _____.

10. She misspelt "accommodation" – that's a _____ mistake.

11. _____ going to the Vatican, what else did you do when you went to Rome?

desert – dessert
A "**desert**" ['dezət] is a barren place with sand *(Wüste)*. It is also a verb meaning "to abandon" *(verlassen, desertieren)*. In this case it is pronounced [dɪ'zɜːt].
The noun "**dessert**" [dɪ'zɜːt] is the sweet course at the end of a meal *(Nachtisch, Dessert)*.

"Fish has mercury, meat has e-coli, veggies have pesticides, desserts cause obesity... so we'll have the 'health-conscious <u>nothing</u> for dinner' special."

everyday – every day
"**Everyday**" *(alltäglich)* is an adjective and should not be confused with "**every day**" *(jeden Tag)*. Look at these examples:
"**Everyday** objects such as knives and forks ..."
"I take my dog for a walk **every day**."

farther – further
Both "**farther**" and "**further**" can be used to refer to physical distance, e.g. "Is it much **farther / further** to our destination?" *(weiter)*. However, only "further" can be used in a figurative sense, e.g. "Are there any **further** questions?".

flat – flatly
"**Flat**" is an adjective and an adverb *(flach)* and should not be confused with "**flatly**" meaning "categorically" *(kategorisch, glatt)*.
"Please put it down **flat** on the floor."
"She **flatly** refused to say anything."

Match each word on the right with the correct sentence on the left.

1. Do you go jogging _____?

    a) desert

2. They were too tired to walk any _____.

    b) dessert

3. There's fruit for _____ tonight.

    c) everyday

4. She made no _____ comment.

    d) every day

5. He _____ denied ever seeing her before.

    e) farther

6. It's very hot in the _____.

    f) further

7. Please stand with your feet _____

   on the floor.

    g) flat

8. Mobile phones are now an accepted part

   of _____ life.

    h) flatly

"Robinson Crusoe's blog – Day 97 · Friday"

Where is Robinson Crusoe?
On a
a) dessert island
b) desert island

hard – hardly

Be careful, the adverb "hardly" has nothing to do with "hard", which is also an adverb as well as an adjective *(hart, schwer)*. "Hardly" means "almost" and has a negative connotation. This means that it is used with negative words such as "any", "anything", "anyone", etc. and with affirmative question tags. Look at these three examples,

"I hardly speak to him anymore."

"I was hardly in a position to disagree with her."

"You can hardly hear what he's saying, can you?"

As you can see from the examples, "hardly" comes before a main verb (with the exception of the verb "to be" which it follows), and after the first modal verb. In addition, if the sentence begins with "hardly", it is followed by the verb and then the subject, e.g. "Hardly had they finished playing football when it began to rain.".

high – highly

Be careful, the adverb "highly" has a different meaning to "high", which is an adjective and an adverb *(hoch)*. "Highly" means "extremely" or "high" in a figurative sense *(äußerst, höchst)*, e.g. "He is highly qualified / respected / gifted.", "She's got a highly paid job in the computer industry.".

late – lately

Be careful, the adverb "lately" *(neulich, in letzter Zeit)* has a different meaning to the adjective and adverb "late" *(spät)*. "Lately" is only used with the present perfect and cannot be used with the past tense (in this case you have to use "recently"), e.g. "Have you seen Jim lately?" but "I saw Jim recently.".

lay – lie

"To lay" *(legen)* and "to lie" *(liegen)* are irregular verbs. Be careful, because the past tense of "to lie" is "lay". Here are two examples:

"She likes lying in bed until midday." *(Note the spelling of lying!)*

"Lay the book flat on the desk."

However, when "to lie" means "to be untruthful" *(lügen)*, it is a regular verb, e.g. "He lied to me about his past.".

Read the following sentences and decide which answer is the correct one in each case.

1. Be careful, this plant is _____ poisonous.

   a) high   b) highly   c) hardly

2. Have you been to the gym _____?

   a) lately   b) hardly

3. They only _____ found out what had happened.

   a) recently   b) lately   c) late

4. Is he telling the truth? Are you sure he's not _____?

   a) lying   b) lies   c) laying

5. If you're not feeling well, go and _____ down.

   a) lay   b) lie   c) lying

6. He's just got a new job and is working very _____.

   a) hardly   b) hard   c) highly

7. I _____ know Jane at all.

   a) hard   b) hardly

8. The trains are all running _____ today.

   a) late   b) lately   c) hardly

9. The bird flew _____ into the air.

   a) highly   b) high

10. They have just finished _____ the carpet.

    a) lying   b) laying

lose – loose
"**To lose**" [luːz] is an irregular verb *(verlieren)*, "I've **lost** my keys.".
"**Loose**" [luːs] is an adjective and means "not tight" *(locker, lose)*, "My shoe is **loose**.". In English you say something "**comes loose**" *(locker werden)*. And be careful, the informal expression "**Get lost!**" means "go away" *(Hau ab!)*.

practice – practise
In *BE* the noun "**practice**" *(Übung, Praxis)* is written with a "c" and the verb "**to practise**" *(üben)* is written with an "s". Both words are pronounced the same way. In *AE* both are usually written with a "c". Remember, "to practise" is followed by the –ing form, e.g. "He **practised parking** backwards before his driving test.".

raise – rise
"**To raise**" ['reɪz] is a transitive verb – it needs a subject and one or more objects – and means "to lift" *(heben, erhöhen)*, e.g. "She **raised** her head when I went in.".
"**To rise**" ['raɪz] is an intransitive verb – it does not have an object – and is irregular. It means "to get up / to come up" *(sich erhöhen, sich erheben, aufgehen)*. Here are a couple of examples:

"The sun **rose** at 5.31 this morning."

"Thank goodness, the temperature **has** finally **risen**!"

Both "**raise**" and "**rise**" can also be used as nouns. "**Rise**" is usually used in the singular and means "increase", either in a literal or figurative sense *(Anstieg, Erhöhung)*, e.g. "The government announced a **rise** in taxes.", "The programme is about the **rise** and fall of Ancient Rome.".
In the US people talk about getting a "**raise**" meaning an increase in their pay *(Gehaltserhöhung)*. British people call this a "pay rise".

sometime – sometimes – some time
"**Sometime**" means "at some point" *(irgendwann)* and should not be confused with the familiar "**sometimes**" *(manchmal)* or "**some time**" *(etwas Zeit)*. Look at these examples:

"We read that book **sometime** last year."

"I **sometimes** read books."

"I need **some time** to think about his offer."

Choose the correct word or expression and complete each of these sentences.

1. You should _____ in front of an audience before you do an audition.

   a) practise to play   b) practice playing   c) practise playing

2. There was a sudden _____ in prices last year.

   a) raise   b) rise   c) rose

3. He's a doctor and has just opened his own _____.

   a) practise   b) practice

4. Last year he spent _____ in Jamaica.

   a) sometimes   b) sometime   c) some time

5. His speech _____ some interesting questions.

   a) raised   b) rose   c) risen

6. I don't know why this screw keeps _____.

   a) coming loose   b) becoming loose   c) becoming lose

7. I think I'll have to go back to the doctor _____ soon.

   a) sometime   b) some time   c) sometimes

8. When the boss came in he _____ to his feet.

   a) raise   b) rise   c) rose

9. I don't believe it – my team _____ again!

   a) has loose   b) has lost   c) has loosed

More easily confused words

There are many German words that have different translations in English depending on what is meant. Some of the ones that commonly cause confusion are given on the following pages with tips on usage.

academic – scholarly – scientific

The German word *"wissenschaftlich"* is often mistranslated. There are three different meanings in English – "scientific", "scholarly" or "academic" – depending on the context. Look at these examples:

"The *New Scientist* magazine reports on scientific issues." *(naturwissenschaftlich)*

"This is a scholarly edition of Shakespeare's plays with footnotes and explanatory texts." (i.e. relating to serious study)

"He has no academic qualifications." (i.e. relating to education)

An "academic" is a teacher at a university. A "scholar" is a specialist in a particular field, especially one to do with the arts. A "scientist" is someone who has expert knowledge of natural or physical science.

ache – hurt
See "Talking about pain" (p. 17)

not allowed – forbidden – prohibited
See "Talking about forbidding something" (p. 87)

appointment – date – deadline

If you "make an appointment" with someone, you have an official meeting with him or her, e.g. "I've made an appointment with my lawyer / bank manager / doctor." *(Termin vereinbaren)*.

When you "set / fix a date" for something then you choose a time for something, e.g. "They've finally set a date for their wedding.".

If you "have a date" with someone or you "go on a date" *(ein Rendezvous haben)*, you arrange to meet someone with whom you are having or starting a relationship, e.g. "Mike and I had a date last week.". In *AE* your "date" is the boy or girl you have agreed to meet and go out with *(Person, mit der man verabredet ist)*.

A "deadline" refers to the date by which something has to be done, e.g. "The deadline for handing in this essay is Monday." *(Abgabetermin, Stichtag)*.

Read the following sentences and decide which answer is the correct one in each case.

1. One of the greatest _____ discoveries of the twentieth century was DNA.

   a) academic   b) scholarly   c) scientific

2. All of the students wore _____ dress to their graduation ceremony.

   a) academic   b) scholarly   c) scientific

3. Shall we fix _____ for our next meeting?

   a) an appointment   b) a date   c) a deadline

4. There is a new law to _____ smoking in public places.

   a) not allow   b) forbid   c) prohibit

5. The _____ for applications is 10th May.

   a) appointment   b) date   c) deadline

6. She made another _____ to see her dentist in six months' time.

   a) appointment   b) date   c) deadline

7. She _____ with Steve yesterday.

   a) had an   b) went on a date   c) had a deadline
      appointment

8. The film studio has finally _____ for the release of their new action film.

   a) made an   b) set a date   c) had a deadline
      appointment

119

audience – onlooker – spectator – viewer

The "**audience**" is a group of people in front of whom a play or concert is performed *(Zuschauer)*. It also refers to the people watching a television programme, a film at the cinema or listening to a speech, e.g. "The **audience** started cheering when he came onto the stage.".

People who watch television are also called "**viewers**", e.g. "This programme is suitable for **viewers** of all ages.". Unlike "audience", "viewer" is a countable noun.

People who watch a sporting event are called "**spectators**".

"**Onlookers**" are people who stop to watch something such as an accident or a fire, e.g. "A crowd of **onlookers** gathered at the scene of the accident.".

aware – conscious

Both "**conscious**" and "**aware**" mean "having knowledge" *(bewusst)*.

But be careful, the adjective "aware" is only used after a verb such as "to be" or "to become" and cannot be used before a noun, e.g. "She was **aware** that she had hurt him.". It is often followed by the preposition "of", e.g. "He became **aware of** the noise.".

"Conscious" can be used before a noun, e.g. "She made a **conscious** effort to be nice.".

In addition, "conscious" also means "being able to see, hear and think" *(bei Bewusstsein)*, e.g. "Even though she had banged her head, she was still **conscious**.".

borrow – lend

See "Talking about lending and borrowing" (p. 51)

"Friends, Romans, Countrymen, lend me your money."

Choose the correct word to fit each of these sentences.

1. The _____ (audience / onlookers / spectators / viewers) gave him a standing ovation after he had finished his speech.

2. He did not have an anaesthetic and so was _____ (conscious / aware) throughout the operation.

3. Most people are _____ (conscious / aware) that it is dangerous to leave a candle burning unattended.

4. Football, rugby and tennis are all _____ (audience / onlooker / spectator / viewer) sports.

5. A lot of _____ (audience / onlookers / spectators / viewers) phoned in to complain about the bad language after the TV show had finished.

6. Can I _____ (borrow / lend) your car tonight?

7. He made a _____ (conscious / aware) decision not to work late every night.

8. A crowd of curious _____ (audience / onlookers / spectators / viewers) gathered in front of the theatre when the car drew up.

9. Would you like me to _____ (borrow / lend) you this book when I've finished reading it?

break – interval – pause

A "**break**" is a short period of time when you stop what you are doing to have a rest *(Pause)*, e.g. "She didn't have a **break** today.".
In *BE* "break" also refers to the period of time between lessons at school, e.g. "At school everyone has to go outside during **break**." (Note there is no definite article!). In *AE* this is called "recess".
If someone goes away for a "break", they go on a short holiday.
The word "**pause**" is used for a break in a conversation of a few seconds, e.g. "There was a short **pause** before Sarah said anything.".
The break in a play, concert or film is called an "**interval**" *(Pause)* or in *AE* "intermission".

countryside – natural environment – nature
See "Talking about nature" (p. 47)

deadly – fatal – lethal

These adjectives have similar meanings but are used with different nouns, so you should learn these collocations:
If something is "**deadly**", it is likely or able to cause death. It is often used with "bite", "disease", "enemy", "poison", "weapon".
If something is "**fatal**", it will cause you to die *(tödlich* – in this case, not to be confused with the German word *fatal)*. It is often used with the following nouns, "accident", "blow (to the head)", "disease", "injury", "wound". It can, however, also be used in a figurative sense to mean "having serious consequences" *(verhängnisvoll, schwerwiegend)*, e.g. "He made a **fatal** mistake.".
If something is "**lethal**", it is very dangerous and able to cause death, however, it suggests a more technical usage. It is commonly used with "amount", "dose", "effect", "injection", "weapon".

drive – journey – ride – trip
See "Talking about trips" (p. 71)

Be careful, the following expressions are different to the German ones: you "**go on a trip / journey**" or "**make a trip / journey**". You "**do a trip / journey in** a certain amount of time", e.g. "I did the **journey** in under two hours.". In *BE* a "**round trip**" is a journey to one or more places and back again, especially if you go a different way there and back *(Rundreise)*. In *AE* it refers to a trip in which you go there and back *(Reise hin und zurück)*.

Choose the correct word from the box to complete each of these sentences.

break – break – countryside – deadly – fatal – interval –
lethal – nature – pause – trip

1. Are they performing the symphony before or after the
   _____ tonight?

2. The _____ in Derbyshire is very varied – there
   are moors, rolling hills, mountains and green fields.

3. There are many _____ poisons, including
   anthrax and cyanide.

4. She took a career _____ so that she could
   travel for a few months.

5. The WWF is a global conservation organization whose initials
   stand for World Wide Fund for _____.

6. I'm going on a business _____ to the US next
   week.

7. The dancers had a half-hour _____ before
   they started the rehearsal.

8. His involvement in the arms scandal dealt a _____
   blow to his election campaign.

9. Some US states execute people by _____ injection.

10. There was an awkward _____ in the conversation
    after she told everyone that she was quitting her job.

economic – economical – economics – economy

"Economics" refers to the study of the production and distribution of goods and services *(Wirtschaftslehre)*. In this case it is followed by a singular verb, e.g. "I'm studying economics – it's really interesting.".

"Economics" can also refer to the financial aspects of something *(Wirtschaftlichkeit)* and in this case it is followed by a plural verb, e.g. "The economics of the government's plan are not very clear.".

The "economy" refers to how a country's trade, industry and finance are organized *(Wirtschaft)*, e.g. "The economy is strong at the moment.".

If something is "economic", it relates to the economy or economics *(wirtschaftlich)*, e.g. "The country was going through a period of economic growth.".

If something is "economical", it means it does not cost a lot of money *(sparsam, günstig)*, e.g. "You should try energy-saving light bulbs – they are much more economical.".

The adverb "economically" is used to show that something relates to the economy, e.g. "The country is going through a difficult time economically.". It can also mean relating to money, e.g. "The project was a success economically.". And finally, to mean with very little waste, "Our heating system does not run very economically.".

fever – temperature

If you use a thermometer to see how hot someone is, you "take their temperature" *(Fieber messen)*. You say a person "has a temperature" or "is running a temperature", e.g. "She has a temperature of 39 (degrees).". Note, in English you say a "temperature of 39°", i.e. the number comes after the word "temperature".

The word "fever" is used to show that someone has a very high temperature, e.g. "She has a fever – her temperature is over 39°.".

"Fever" can also be used in a figurative sense to mean "nervous excitement", e.g. "She was in a fever of excitement all day.".

finished – ready

If you are "ready", then you are prepared to do something *(fertig im Sinne von bereit)*, e.g. "Are you ready to go?". "Ready" is often followed by the preposition "for", e.g. "It's time to get ready for bed.".

"Finished" is used if something is "over" *(fertig im Sinne von abgeschlossen, erledigt)*, e.g. "Have you finished your homework?".

The German expression *"fix und fertig"* is translated as "exhausted".

Read the following sentences and decide which answer is the correct one in each case.

1. The Welsh _____ (economics / economy) is dominated by the service sector.

2. This is a very _____ (economic / economical) meal – it's made with very simple ingredients.

3. Her _____ (fever / temperature) is slightly raised, but it's nothing serious.

4. The country's _____ (economic / economical) policy has recently come in for a lot of criticism.

5. I'm hungry – will lunch be _____ (ready / finished) soon?

6. Harvard University has a very prestigious Department of _____ (Economics / Economy).

7. She took the boy's _____ (fever / temperature).

8. Have you _____ (ready / finished) writing that report yet?

9. The government recently published a report on the _____ (economics / economy) of climate change.

to fit – to match – to suit

"To fit" is used to show that something is the right size *(passen)*, e.g. "This dress is just the right size – it fits perfectly.", "The table fits nicely between the window and the bookcase.".

It cannot be used in the progressive with this meaning. "To fit" is regular in *BE* and usually irregular in *AE* (fit – fit – fit).

If something "matches" something else, it goes with it *(passen)*, e.g. "That dress matches your eyes." (Note, unlike in German there is no preposition!). As with "to fit", it cannot be used in the progressive.

The verb "to suit" means that the colour or style of something is good, e.g. "That dress really suits you." *(steht dir)*. This verb cannot be used in the progressive either.

"To suit" can also mean "to be suitable for" *(passen im Sinne von geeignet sein)*, e.g. "You need to find a job that suits your personality.", "What day suits you for our meeting?".

Be careful, the German expression "*jdm. passt es nicht, dass / wie*" is translated as "to not like something", e.g. "I don't like your tone of voice." *(dein Ton passt mir nicht)*.

ill – sick

The adjectives "sick" and "ill" both mean "not well". However, in *BE* they are used differently: "sick" is used before a noun, but "ill" is used after a noun, e.g. "He is looking after his sick mother. She is very ill.".

"Ill" can be used before a noun if qualified by an adverb, e.g. "a terminally ill patient" *(todkrank)*. Other common adverb combinations include "seriously ill" *(ernsthaft krank)*, "gravely / dangerously ill" *(ernsthaft krank)* and "mentally ill" *(geisteskrank)*.

A person "falls ill" or "is taken ill" *(krank werden)*.

Be careful, Americans use the word "sick" to mean someone is ill and does not feel well, e.g. "She can't go to school today – she's sick.".

In *BE* the expression "to be sick" means "to vomit" *(sich übergeben)*.

"The sick" is used to refer to people who are ill, e.g. "Nurses care for the sick.".

Choose one of the words explained on the opposite page to complete each of these sentences. Use the verb in the correct tense.

1. These gloves don't _____ very well – they're a bit too small.

2. Sue's been on _____ leave since the end of January.

3. Do you think the sofa will _____ over there?

4. That colour really _____ you – it _____ the blue of your eyes.

5. I think I'm going to be _____ – could you stop the car, please?

6. This applicant doesn't really _____ our needs.

7. A hospice is a place which provides care for _____ and people who are terminally _____.

"I just shook his hand and he was sick."

to notice – to realize – to recognize

If you "notice" something, then you become aware of something with one of your five senses *(bemerken)*, e.g. "She noticed that he hadn't washed his hands.".

If you "realize" something, you know and understand it *(erkennen, begreifen)*, e.g. "She realized that she'd upset him.".

If you "recognize" someone, you know the person because you have seen or heard him or her before *(wiedererkennen)*, e.g. "I hardly recognized her now that she's got short hair!".

"To notice", "to realize" and "to recognize" are not usually used in the progressive.

politics – policy
See "Talking about politics" (p. 23)

road – street
See "Talking about streets and roads" (p. 35)

shade – shadow

"Shade" refers to an area where there is no sunlight *(Schatten)*. In this meaning it is uncountable. If you mean a specific area, then you talk about "a patch of shade" or "an area of shade" *(ein schattiger Platz)*.

"A shade" is something that protects you from the light or sun, e.g. "a lampshade" *(Lampenschirm)*.

A "shadow" is the black shape created when an object blocks out the light *(Schatten)*. Look at these two examples:

"It's too hot in the sun, let's go and sit in the shade."

"The dog was chasing the boy's shadow."

If you "shadow" someone, you follow the person secretly *(beschatten)*.

And remember, "shadow" is used to show the position members of the UK Parliament would hold if their party were in power, e.g. "The Shadow Foreign Secretary" *(Schattenaußenminister/in)*.

What's on the wall?
a) shade
b) a shadow

Choose the correct word or expression and complete each of these sentences. Use the verb in the correct tense.

1. The police officer _____ him from the description she had received.

   a) to notice   b) to realize   c) to recognize

2. The number of _____ accidents has increased over the past few years.

   a) road   b) street

3. Can you move, please? You're casting a _____ over my book.

   a) shade   b) shadow

4. We have a new company _____ on the use of mobile phones.

   a) politics   b) policy

5. I _____ how tired I was till I sat down.

   a) to notice   b) to realize   c) to recognize

6. Homeless people often live on the _____.

   a) roads   b) streets

7. If he doesn't win the next election, he's going to retire from

   _____.

   a) politics   b) policy

8. It's better to sit in the _____ than in the sun.

   a) shade   b) shadow

False friends

False friends are words which look the same or very similar in German and English. They do not, however, have the same meaning. How can you tell if a word is a false friend or not? One thing you can do is to see if the translation fits the context, especially if you are trying to work out the meaning of an English word. Look at the following example: "He gave his girlfriend a very expensive birthday gift.". It is most unlikely that the German word "*Gift*" is meant!
The best thing to do is to learn some of the most common ones to avoid making mistakes.

actual
What were his **actual** words?

eigentlich, tatsächlich
Was hat er tatsächlich gesagt?

to blame s.o. for s.th.
He **blamed himself for** it.

jdm. die Schuld für etw. geben
Er gab sich die Schuld dafür.

brave
She **bravely** faced death.

mutig, tapfer
Sie sah dem Tod mutig ins Gesicht.

chef
This **chef** makes great food.

Koch / Köchin
Dieser Koch kocht hervorragend.

confession
He made a **confession**.
I have a **confession** to make.

Geständnis, Beichte
Er hat ein Geständnis abgelegt.
Ich muss etwas beichten.

critic
The **critic** was invited to the film premiere.

Kritiker/in
Der Kritiker wurde zur Filmpremiere eingeladen.

eventually
After a long journey she **eventually** arrived.

letztendlich, schließlich
Nach einer langen Reise kam sie schließlich an.

notice
Have you read the **notice**?

Aushang, Bekanntmachung
Hast du den Aushang gelesen?

receipt
When you buy something you should keep the **receipt**.

Quittung
Wenn du etwas kaufst, solltest du die Quittung aufbewahren.

sensible
That's a very **sensible** thing to do.

vernünftig
Es ist sehr vernünftig, das zu machen.

Read each of the following sentences carefully. The context will
enable you to choose the correct German word to explain the
words in bold.

1. The coat was made of a very soft **fabric**.
   a) *Stoff*   b) *Fabrik*

2. You should take a **tablet** every four hours to ease the pain.
   a) *Tablett*   b) *Tablette*

3. The chemical **formula** for water is H_2O.
   a) *Formular*   b) *Formel*   c) *Form*

4. We had a great holiday in Tuscany – we spent a lot of time just
   wandering around the towns and watching the locals.
   a) *wandern*   b) *schlendern*

5. How much **rent** do you pay every month?
   a) *Rente*   b) *Rentner*   c) *Miete*

6. A new football **stadium** is being built.
   a) *Stadium*   b) *Stadion*

7. They are **engaged** and are getting married next summer.
   a) *engagiert*   b) *verlobt*

8. Please fill out the **form** and sign it on the back.
   a) *Formel*   b) *Form*   c) *Formular*

9. The museum is open to the **public** every day from 10 a.m. to
   5 p.m.
   a) *Publikum*   b) *Öffentlichkeit*

10. The **murder** took place on a dark night in January.
    a) *Mord*   b) *Mörder*

11. Are you wearing a **vest** underneath your shirt?
    a) *Weste*   b) *Unterhemd*

Here are some German words which can cause confusion.

Ambulanz
Die Klinik hat eine große
Ambulanz mit 9 Zimmern.

outpatient clinic / department
The hospital has a large **outpatient clinic** with 9 rooms.

aktuell
Die aktuelle Uhrzeit ist 10:49.
Der Film ist sehr aktuell.
Aktuelle Informationen!

current, topical, up-to-date
The **current** time is 10.49.
The film is very **topical**.
Up-to-date information!

sich blamieren
Er hat sich vor der ganzen
Familie blamiert.

to make a fool of o.s.
He **made a fool of himself in front of** all the family.

brav
Beim Essen war das Kind sehr
brav.

well-behaved
The child was very **well-behaved** during the meal.

Chef/in
Er mochte seinen Chef nicht.

boss
He did not like his **boss**.

eventuell
Ich rufe eventuell später an.

possibly
I may **possibly** phone later.

Fabrik
Sie arbeiten in einer Fabrik.

factory
They work in a **factory**.

Konfession
Welche Konfession haben Sie?

denomination
Which **denomination** are you?

Kritik
Er kann keine Kritik vertragen.
Gestern stand eine Kritik über
den Film in der Zeitung.

criticism, review
He is very sensitive to **criticism**.
There was a **review** of the film in yesterday's newspaper.

Notiz
Ich werde mir Notizen machen.

note
I'll take **notes**.

Rezept
Hast du ein Rezept für Kekse?
Der Arzt muss dir ein Rezept
ausstellen.

recipe, prescription
Do you have a **recipe** for biscuits?
The doctor has to write you a **prescription**.

sensibel
Sei nicht so sensibel!

sensitive
Don't be so **sensitive**!

Stadium
Der Krebs wurde im frühen
Stadium entdeckt.

stage
The cancer was detected at an early **stage**.

Translate the German words to complete each of the following sentences. In case you need some help, the English words are given at the bottom of the page.

1. This subject is very _____ (aktuell).

2. He behaved in a very loud and _____ (ordinär) manner.

3. Many young people today are very _____ (engagiert) and do volunteering for a year.

4. Although the _____ (Kritiker) wrote an unfavourable _____ (Kritik) of the film, the _____ (Publikum) appeared to enjoy it.

5. In this film the _____ (Mörder) kills his victim by putting _____ (Gift) in the tea which the butler takes up to him on a _____ (Tablett) at 8 o'clock every morning.

6. A _____ (Rentner) is a person who has retired and collects a _____ (Rente). In the US they are called retirees.

7. In Britain men often wear a _____ (Weste) at formal weddings.

audience	committed	critic	vulgar
murderer	pension	pensioner	poison
review	topical	tray	waistcoat

Singular or plural?

Here are a few general reminders:

- Remember that some nouns might look plural but they have a singular verb, e.g. "**news**", "**the United Nations**", "**the United States**", e.g. "The **news** about her mother **is** very shocking.".
- Words that end in "**-ics**" like "**physics**", "**aerobics**", "**economics**", "**gymnastics**", "**athletics**" and "**mathematics**" are generally used with a singular verb, e.g. "**Athletics is** my favourite sport.".
- Some singular nouns can also be used with plural verbs and pronouns, e.g. "**team**", "**family**", "**government**", "**staff**", etc. if the emphasis is more on the individuals than the whole. Look at these two sentences, "The **team are** very happy that they won the match." (every member of the team), but "This **government wants** to improve healthcare." (here the emphasis is on the government as a whole).

Countable or uncountable – difference in meaning

Some nouns can be both countable and uncountable, depending on the meaning. Look at these examples:

> "Mirrors are made of **glass**."
> "Can I have **a glass** of water, please?"

In the first example, the word "glass" refers to the material out of which the mirrors are made. In the second one, it refers to a specific item which is countable. The same rule also applies to the following nouns: "**paper**", "**iron**", "**rubber**", "**stone**", "**brick**" and "**cloth**".

Likewise, if you are referring to an idea or thing in general or something abstract, then it is uncountable. Look at how the meaning of the word "people" changes in these two sentences:

> "The **people** here are very friendly." *(Leute)*
> "The Incas were **an ancient people**." *(Volk)*

(And remember, "people" is always followed by a plural verb even if it is used with the indefinite article, e.g. "The Irish are a people who have a difficult history.".)

Other common nouns that can either be countable or uncountable include: **work** – **life** – **drink** – **hair** – **light** – **land** – **noise** – **room** – **experience** – **time** – **trade** – **home** – **policy** – **youth**.

Some words to do with food can also be uncountable or countable, such as "**cake**", "**pepper**", "**chocolate**" and "**fish**". Drinks are usually uncountable, e.g. "I like **coffee**.". But if you are thinking of a cup or glass, it is countable, e.g. "What would you like to drink?" – "I'd like **a coffee**, please.".

Fill in each blank with "a" or "an" if the noun following the blank is used as a countable noun, or leave the blank empty if the noun is used as an uncountable noun. Then translate the underlined word into German.

1. a) For this recipe you need _____ red <u>pepper</u>.

   b) Can you pass the salt and _____ <u>pepper</u> please?

2. a) Have you got _____ <u>iron</u>? I need to press my trousers.

   b) The bridge is made of _____ <u>iron</u> and steel.

3. a) What _____ <u>noise</u>! Please could you all be quiet!

   b) She's got very good hearing and is rather sensitive to

      _____ <u>noise</u>.

4. a) Sue's just finished university and is now looking for

      _____ <u>work</u>.

   b) Beethoven's Ninth Symphony is _____ very famous <u>work</u>.

5. a) The police arrested _____ <u>youth</u> in connection with the break-in.

   b) _____ <u>youth</u> is the period between childhood and adulthood.

6. a) _____ <u>paper</u> can be made of wood or cloth.

   b) She has just written _____ <u>paper</u> on diabetes.

7. a) This blog covers _____ American foreign <u>policy</u>.

   b) The government has _____ new <u>policy</u> on education.

8. a) Many immigrants to the US believed it to be _____ <u>land</u> of plenty.

   b) This is _____ bad <u>land</u> for farming – it's very dry.

9. a) Many Irish people decided to start _____ new <u>life</u> in America.

   b) What do scientists know about _____ <u>life</u> on Mars?

10. a) Many people believe that _____ <u>trade</u> in endangered species must be stopped.

    b) Supermarkets are now doing _____ roaring <u>trade</u> in organic food.

135

Prepositions in fixed expressions

Prepositions often cause learners of English, or indeed other languages, problems. A good dictionary or grammar book will enable you to understand their basic different meanings – many of which will already be familiar.

The purpose of this study point is to help you learn fixed expressions with different prepositions. The correct use of these expressions will improve your English. But be careful, although some of them might look similar to the German expression, in almost all of the cases a different preposition is used. You will have to learn each expression as a fixed unit – example sentences and tips on usage have been given to help you. The list contains some of the more common and most important expressions.

at
The food at that restaurant is **at best** mediocre, **at worst** inedible! *(bestenfalls), (schlimmstenfalls)*
You can also just use one part of the expression, e.g. "At best we'll only have to pay back the deposit.".

The missing jewels must be discovered **at all costs**. *(um jeden Preis)*

She talked about her holdiay **at length**. *(ausführlich)*
You can also say "at great length".

It was love **at first sight**. *(auf den ersten Blick)*

He organized a meeting **at her request**. *(auf Bitten von jdm.)*
Similar expressions include "at s.o.'s suggestion" (auf Anregung von jdm.) *and "at s.o.'s expense"* (auf Kosten von jdm.).

Queen Elizabeth II ascended the throne **at the age of** 25. *(im Alter von)*

Users of the Internet remain **at risk** from viruses. *(in Gefahr)*
The verb "to put" is often used before this expression, e.g. "to put s.o. / s.th. at risk". You will also often see "at great risk".

At the risk of being boring, I'm going to bed now. *(auf die Gefahr hin)*
Remember, this expression is always followed by the –ing form.

Choose expressions from the left-hand page to complete the following sentences. In one or two cases more than one answer may be possible.

1. He rescued the dog _____ to himself.

2. She was determined to win the race _____.

3. In Britain you can learn to drive _____ 17.

4. A suspect was questioned _____ by the police about his movements on the night of the murder.

5. Their eyes met across the room and as they both said later, it was love _____.

6. Journalists who go to disaster areas do so _____ to themselves.

7. Steve, my boss, is always very keen for us to go to conferences. In fact, it was _____ that I attended the one on Web 2.0.

8. _____ being considered old-fashioned, I think it is good when a man opens a door for a woman.

9. She laughed at the joke even though it was made _____ _____.

by

I was there **by accident / chance**. *(per Zufall)*
*You can also say "**by pure chance**" (rein zufällig). A similar expression is "**by mistake**"* (aus Versehen).

You have to wash this **by hand**. *(mit der / von Hand)*

I learnt the poem **by heart**. *(auswendig)*

You don't need any help – you can finish that **by yourself**. *(allein)*

By the way, would you like to go out tonight? *(übrigens)*
This expression should not be used in essays or speeches as it is rather informal.

The preposition "by" is also used in the following expressions:
"**day by day**" *(Tag für Tag)*, "**step by step**" *(Schritt für Schritt)*, "**side by side**" *(Seite an Seite)* and "**one by one**" *(einer nach dem anderen)*.

for

Shall we go this way **for a change**? *(zur Abwechslung)*
Note in English there is an indefinite article.

We're reading this **for fun**. *(aus Spaß)*

I'm not doing this **for my sake** but **for your sake**. *(um meinet-, deinetwillen)*
*The expression "**for goodness sake**" (also "**for Heaven's sake**", "**for God's sake**") is used for emphasis* (um Himmelswillen).

For sale *(Zum Verkauf)*
You often see signs saying this outside houses in Britain.

I'm forwarding this message **for your information**. *(zur Information / Kenntnisnahme)*
*It is often abbreviated to "**FYI**" in e-mails or text messages. The expression can also be used in spoken English to tell someone that they are wrong about something, e.g. "**For your information**, I didn't send him that mail!".*

from

From now on you can go to school by bike. *(ab jetzt)*
*A variation on this expression can be used for the past "**from then on**"* (seitdem).

He played the piece **from memory**. *(auswendig)*

Choose the correct expression from the box to complete each of these sentences.

> day by day – side by side – by chance – by hand – by heart –
> by yourself – for a change – for fun – for goodness sake –
> for your information – from then on

1. _____, stop making such a fuss!

2. The victim's health improved _____.

3. He saw a programme about the effects of global warming.
   _____ he decided not to travel by car but to
   go by bike.

4. She didn't need any music – she played the piece _____.

5. She found the book _____ – she had
   forgotten that she still had it.

6. _____, I would never have done anything like
   that!

7. They walked down the street _____, holding
   hands.

8. You can't be serious – you read that _____?!

9. Can we have yoghurt for breakfast today _____?

10. We don't have a dishwasher – you'll have to do the washing-up
    _____.

11. You'll have to do it _____ – I haven't got time
    to help you today.

in

In addition to acting in the film, he also produced it. *(neben, zusätzlich)*
"To" can either be followed by a noun or a verb in the –ing form.

They've sold out of tickets. **In any case**, the film's meant to be boring. *(sowieso)*
You will also hear "in any event". Neither expression should be used in essays or speeches as they are informal.

In case of bad weather, the match will be held indoors. *(im Falle)*

In conclusion, I would like to say that … *(zum Schluss)*
This expression is good for summing up your ideas and arguments at the end of an essay or speech.

We talked about this topic **in depth**. *(gründlich)*
There is also an adjective "in-depth", e.g. "an in-depth discussion". A similiar expression is "in detail" (ausführlich).

Everyone thought she was wrong. But **in fact**, she was right. *(tatsächlich, in der Tat)*
You can also say "in actual fact".

He planted a tree **in memory of** his grandmother. *(zur Erinnerung an)*
This expression is used when you do something to remember someone who has died. A related expression is "in honour of" which can either be used for a person or a thing (zu Ehren einer Person / einer Sache).

In theory, everyone works 35 hours a week. However, **in practice** we all work at least 40 hours. *(theoretisch), (in der Praxis)*
In English there is no definite article with either expression. Note the spelling of "practice".

She arrived **in time** to see the beginning. *(rechtzeitig)*
You can also say "just in time" (gerade noch rechtzeitig).

Everyone answered **in turn**. *(der Reihe nach)*

In view of the circumstances, we should cancel our meeting. *(angesichts)*

off

He was quoted **off the record**. *(im Vertrauen, inoffiziell)*
"Record" is pronounced ['rekɔːd]. *The opposite is "on the record".*

Complete the following sentences using expressions from the opposite page.

1. They got there just _____ to see him score a goal.

2. His father taught David to play the violin and David then taught his son _____.

3. _____ two sons, they also have one daughter.

4. Let's go through this plan _____ to make sure we all know what we're doing.

5. Beethoven composed his third symphony _____ Napoleon.

6. He's a good teacher. _____, he's one of the best I've ever had.

7. _____ I would like to say that I am against genetic engineering. But you mustn't print that!

on

How much water should we drink a day **on average**? *(im Durchschnitt)*

I would like to thank you **on behalf of** everyone. *(im Namen von)*

I'll come **on condition that** you let me drive. *(unter der Bedingung, dass)*
"That" is sometimes omitted.

Are you going by car or **on foot**? *(zu Fuß)*

These DVDs are **on offer** at the moment. *(im Angebot)*
You will often also see "on special offer".

I don't go to zoos **on principle**. *(aus Prinzip)*
Note the spelling of "princip_le_".

Was that an accident or did you do it **on purpose**? *(absichtlich)*

On the contrary, I actually liked his last film. *(im Gegenteil)*

I read about it **on the Internet**. *(im Internet)*

He wasn't late today, he got here **on time**. *(pünktlich)*

out of

When he got on the bus he was completely **out of breath**. *(außer Atem)*
"Out of" is also translated as "außer" in the following expressions: "out of hand" (außer Kontrolle), *"out of order"* (außer Betrieb), *"out of reach"* (außer Reichweite). *Note there is a definite article in the expression "out of the question"* (außer Frage).

That expression is **out of date**. *(veraltet, altmodisch)*
A similar expression is "out of fashion" (aus der Mode).

I haven't spoken French for ages – I'm **out of practice**. *(aus der Übung)*
Note the spelling of "practi_ce_".

to

To some extent, I'd have to agree with you. *(in gewissem Maße, zum Teil)*
You can also say "to a certain extent". A related expression is "to a great extent" (in hohem Maße).

Choose the correct expression to complete each of these
sentences.

on average – on foot – on principle – on purpose – on time –
on the Internet – out of fashion – out of practice –
out of reach – out of the question – to a certain extent

1. He walks five miles a day _____.

2. Medicine should always be kept _____
   of children.

3. There is a wealth of information _____.

4. The criticism of his latest novel was valid _____.

5. There were a lot of delays at the airport yesterday – did your
   plane leave _____?

6. He says it's quicker to go there _____
   than by bike.

7. I'm afraid that's quite _____ – I refuse to
   do that _____!

8. I'll play tennis – but I'm afraid I'm _____.

9. The authorities are not sure whether the forest fires were started
   _____ or not.

10. Corsets went _____ a long time ago.

under

A new car park is **under construction**. *(im Bau)*
This is a more formal expression – you will often see it on the Internet.

I was **under the impression** that you knew the answer. *(den Eindruck haben)*

Under no circumstances may pupils eat in the classrooms! *(unter keinen Umständen)*
Note that if this expression is at the beginning of the sentence, it is followed by the verb then the subject.

Plans are currently **under way** to open a new museum. *(in der Mache)*

up to

I agree with you **up to a point**. *(bis zu einem gewissen Grad)*

Is this website really **up-to-date**? *(auf dem neuesten Stand)*
*This expression is also sometimes spelt "**up to date**".*

with

With regard to your letter of 19ᵗʰ October, ... *(in Bezug auf)*
This is a formal expression.

With the exception of the Foreign Secretary all of the Cabinet was present. *(mit Ausnahme von)*
Note, the English expression has a definite article.

without

This is **without doubt** the best thing you've ever written. *(ohne Zweifel)*
*This expression is used for emphasis. You can also say "**without a doubt**".*
*A similar expression is "**without exception**"* (ohne Ausnahme).

Complete the following sentences using prepositions from this chapter.

1. They wrote this book _____ memory _____ their father.

2. Did you do this picture _____ yourself? –
   No, I found it _____ the Internet.

3. _____ her request, no questions were asked.

4. What about watching this _____ a change?

5. This machine should work _____ theory.

6. _____ no circumstances can we accept this kind of behaviour – it's completely _____ order!

7. It's a shame you didn't like the film. –
   _____ the contrary, I enjoyed it very much!

8. This is _____ doubt the best meal I've ever had!

9. _____ view _____ what's just happened, I think we should all go out and celebrate.

10. Is this house _____ sale?

11. _____ now on we'll have to meet at my house.

12. The man got out of the house just _____ time – seconds later the roof fell in.

13. _____ the way, what time are they coming tonight?

14. I was _____ the impression that the museum was closed today.

Phrasal verbs

Phrasal verbs are very common, especially in spoken English. They often cause problems because their meaning cannot be guessed from the individual words. This is because a simple verb – such as "come", "get", "go", "take" – is combined with a preposition (or adverb) to form an expression with a completely different meaning. It is often impossible to work out the meaning. This is why it is best to learn each phrasal verb as an individual expression and in a context.

Some phrasal verbs have several meanings. Look at these sentences with "**to go on**". Which meaning fits which sentence?	
1. If you touch this, the light goes on.	a) continue
2. What's going on over there?	b) last
3. Sorry, I interrupted – do go on.	c) pass
4. The meeting went on till 6 p.m.	d) happen
5. As time went on, things got worse.	e) light up

In a formal context (e.g. writing an essay), it is better to avoid using certain phrasal verbs. Many of them have a formal equivalent, others have to be paraphrased. In the "Topics" section there are phrasal verbs to do with different subjects. On the following pages you will find some more. Be careful, if there is no note to the contrary, the position of the preposition or adverb cannot be changed! Formal equivalents are given in brackets and a "*" means the phrasal verb is informal.

bring

to bring s.o. (a)round   *(to persuade s.o. to agree with you)*
He finally managed to **bring** her **around**.

to bring s.th. back   *(to re-introduce)*
I'm glad they haven't **brought back** the death penalty in Britain.
The object can go before or after "back".

to bring s.o. / s.th. down   *(to remove s.o. / s.th. from power)*
The latest scandal almost **brought down** the government.
The object can go before or after "down".

to bring s.th. out   *(to release s.th., to launch s.th.)*
They have just **brought out** a new mobile phone.
The object can go before or after "out".

to bring s.o. up   *(to raise s.o.)*
I was born in London but **brought up** in Berlin.
This phrasal verb is often used in the passive.

Here are two more phrasal verbs with "go" which have several meanings. Choose the meaning which you think fits in each case – remember to use the right tense!

> to be attracted to s.o. – to attack s.o. – to try to get s.th. – to choose, have s.th. – to like (a particular thing)

1. I don't *go for _____ thrillers – I prefer action films.

2. The dog *went for _____ the postman and tried to bite him.

3. He *went for _____ the ball but unfortunately he missed it.

4. He's much older than her, isn't he? She seems to *go for

   _____ older men.

5. I think I'll *go for _____ the soup.

> to set – to stop working – to be remembered, recorded – to sink – to decrease

6. The price of computers has **gone down** _____ dramatically over the past few years.

7. The sun **goes down** _____ early in December.

8. The ship **went down** _____ in a terrible storm.

9. My computer **went down** _____ three times yesterday – I think it's got a virus.

10. She will **go down** _____ as the first female president.

Phrasal verbs

come

to come across s.o. / s.th.   *(to meet s.o. or find s.th. by chance)*
I **came across** it in a second-hand bookshop.

to come into s.th.   *(to start s.th., to inherit s.th.)*
These plants **come into** flower in May. *(start flowering)*
When his grandmother died, he **came into** a lot of money. *(inherited)*

to come to s.th.   *(to reach s.th.)*
They **came to** an agreement very quickly.

to come up against s.th.   *(to encounter difficulties or problems)*
The local government **came up against** a great deal of opposition to its housing plans.

do

*to do away with s.th.   *(to abolish s.th., to get rid of s.th.)*
Britain **did away with** the death penalty for murder in 1965.

*to do s.th. up   *(to renovate or redecorate s.th.)*
After they bought the house they spent a year **doing** it **up** before they finally moved in.
The object can go before or after "up".

to do without s.th.   *(to manage without s.th.)*
I haven't got any milk – we'll have to **do without** today.

get

to get s.th. across to s.o.   *(to make s.o. understand s.th.)*
He found it difficult to **get** his idea **across** to his boss.
The object can go before or after "across".

to get by   *(to manage with difficulty to live or do s.th.)*
When we were young we just had enough money to **get by**.
This phrasal verb is intransitive so it does not have an object.

to get s.o. down   *(to make s.o. miserable, to depress s.o.)*
The cold and wet weather in November really **gets me down**.

to get into s.th.   *(to become interested in s.th.)*
I'm really **getting into** jazz.

to get out of (doing) s.th.   *(to avoid (doing) s.th.)*
She always tries to **get out of** helping with the chores.

The phrasal verbs "to come out" and "to get at" both have several meanings. Choose the meaning which you think fits best in each case – remember to use the right tense!

> to disappear (after being washed) – to be published –
> to appear – to tell people you are gay

1. She **came out** _____ at university and has been living with Susan ever since.
2. I've tried everything, but this stain just won't **come out** _____.
3. Her latest book **came out** _____ at the end of last year.
4. The sun **came out** _____ from behind the cloud.

> to reach s.th. – to imply – to discover s.th. – to criticize s.o.

5. What's she *getting at** _____? I don't understand her!
6. My mum's always *getting at** _____ me for not tidying up.
7. I can't *get at** _____ that book up there – can you help me, please?
8. Many people believe that we still have not **got at** _____ the truth behind JFK's murder.

go

to go along with s.th. / s.o.   *(to agree with s.th. / s.o.)*
Although I didn't really like the suggestion I **went along with** it.

to go back on s.th.   *(to break a promise)*
The government has **gone back on** its promise not to raise taxes.

*to go down with s.th.   *(to fall ill, but not seriously ill)*
She's **gone down with** a cold.
This phrasal verb is mainly used in BE. It is often used in the present progressive or in the present perfect. Be careful, with "I" you use "come" instead of "go".

*to go on at s.o.   *(to criticize s.o., to nag s.o.)*
She keeps **going on at** me about the clothes I wear.

make

to make for s.o. / s.th.   *(to move towards s.o. / s.th.)*
He went through the door and **made for** the sofa.

to make off   *(to leave in a hurry)*
The thief **made off** as soon as he heard the door open.
This verb is intransitive so it does not have an object.

to make s.th. over to s.o.   *(to transfer ownership of s.th. to s.o. else)*
He had no children so he **made** his house **over to** his niece.
The direct object can go before or after "over".
If you have or are given a "makeover", your appearance is changed, e.g. "Some reality TV programmes are about people who have makeovers.".

to make up for s.th.   *(to compensate for s.th.)*
They took her some flowers to **make up for** being late.

put

to put s.th off   *(to postpone s.th.)*
We had to **put** the meeting **off** until tomorrow.
You can also say "to put off doing s.th.". If you "put s.o. off", you cancel or postpone your appointment with them.

to be put off (doing) s.th.   *(to make s.o. not want to do s.th.)*
I saw a programme on battery farms – it really **put** me **off** eating eggs.

to put up with s.th.   *(to endure s.th.)*
I left because I couldn't **put up with** their complaints any longer.

The phrasal verbs "to make up" and "to put down" both have
several meanings. Choose the meaning which you think fits best
in each case. Remember to use the right tense and change the
word order if necessary!

> to put cosmetics on – to find (the rest of a sum of money) –
> to be friends again (after an argument) – to invent s.th.

1. We often argue but we always **make up** _____

   before we go to sleep.

2. She often **makes up** _____ stories and poems.

3. She **made up** _____ her face before the party.

4. I'm paying £50 and my father's **making up** _____

   the rest.

> to criticize (especially in front of others) – to attribute –
> to kill (an animal because it is old or hurt) – to suppress –
> to enter in a list (*here:* in the list)

5. They **put** his mistakes **down** _____ to

   inexperience.

6. They had to have the cat **put down** _____

   after the accident.

7. Have you **put** your name **down** _____ for

   the school trip to London?

8. The troops **put down** _____ the rebellion.

9. She's jealous of me and always **puts** me **down** _____

   in front of other people.

set

to set s.th. aside *(to reserve s.th., usu. money)*
He **set aside** some money every month for his pension.
The object can go before or after "aside".
The phrasal verb "to put aside" has the same meaning.

to set s.th. aside *(to ignore s.th., usu. negative feelings)*
They decided to **set aside** their differences and start again.
The object can go before or after "aside".

to set s.th. back *(to hinder, to slow down the progress of s.th.)*
Scientists say new laws threaten to **set** research **back** several years.
The object can go before or after "back".
The noun "setback" (Rückschlag) comes from this phrasal verb, e.g. "They suffered many setbacks.".

*to set s.o. back s.th. *(to cost s.o. s.th.)*
My new computer **set** me **back** £600.

to set s.th. forth *(to propose s.th., to present s.th. clearly)*
He **set forth** his ideas in a presentation.
The object can go before or after "forth". This phrasal verb is formal.
"To set forth" can also be used in a literary sense to mean "to start a journey", e.g. "He set forth on his travels.". In this case it is intransitive so it does not have an object.

take

to take after s.o. *(to resemble s.o.)*
He **takes after** his father.
This phrasal verb is never used in the progressive.

to take s.th. back *(to retract s.th. you have said)*
I **take back** what I just said.
The object can go before or after "back".
To "take s.th. back", can also mean to return unsatisfactory goods to a shop, e.g. "I took the damaged book back to the shop.".

to take over s.th. *(to assume control of s.th.)*
An international company **took over** the smaller one.
A person can "take over as", e.g. "He took over as manager when she left.".

to take s.o. up on s.th. *(to accept s.o.'s offer or invitation)*
I decided to **take** her **up on** her offer of a lift.

The phrasal verbs "to set off" and "to take up" both have several meanings. Choose the meaning which you think fits best in each case. Remember to use the right tense and change the word order if necessary!

> to make s.th. explode – to cause (s.th. to happen) –
>
> to begin one's journey – to make s.o. start to laugh a lot

1. The joke about the elephant and the flea always **set** him **off** _____.

2. They are worried that new road taxes could **set off** _____ mass protests.

3. They **set off** _____ early to avoid the rush hour.

4. The terrorists **set off** _____ a bomb.

> to consume (time) – to start doing s.th. regularly –
> to shorten s.th. – to start (a job) – to fill (space)

5. She decided to **take up** _____ yoga.

6. He **took up** _____ a new job in Hong Kong.

7. These trousers are too long – I'm afraid you'll have to **take** them **up** _____.

8. He promised not to **take up** _____ too much of his time.

9. These shelves **take up** _____ very little space.

Idioms

An idiom is a fixed expression which has a meaning that is often not clear or obvious. Look at this example, "**They got on like a house on fire.**". The meaning of the idiom is different to that of the individual words, so translating the expression word for word will not necessarily mean that you understand the idiom. However, the context will often help you to do so. Look at the expression again in context and decide which meaning you think is the most likely:

"**They got on like a house on fire.** At the party they just sat in a corner talking and laughing all night."
❑ to be cross   ❑ to argue   ❑ to get on very well

Some idioms can be deceptive. Look at this example, "**I've got itchy feet.**". Although it could literally mean that someone's feet are itching, the idiom itself means something different. Again, the context will help you to understand the meaning.

"**I've got itchy feet** listening to you talk about your trip round the world. It's about time I went on another trip."
❑ I want to scratch   ❑ I want to travel   ❑ I want to sit down

> **a hidden agenda**
> a secret reason for doing s.th. in order to gain an advantage

"I've got a board meeting in ten minutes and I can't find my hidden agenda!"

Do not try to translate German idioms into English (or vice versa) – this could cause confusion and also be comical. The English version of the German idiom "*aus einer Mücke einen Elefanten machen*" has nothing to do with mosquitoes or elephants! The English equivalent is "**to make a mountain out of a molehill**".

1. Underline the idiom in each sentence. Then find the correct meaning in the box – the context will help you.

> **to just manage to avoid trouble or danger – to feel ill – to organize o.s. – to try to avoid being caught**

1. I've been feeling under the weather recently. – Then you should go and see a doctor. _____

2. He escaped from prison a month ago and has been on the run ever since. _____

3. The driver had a narrow escape when his car crashed – he was not hurt. _____

4. I can't decide which film to go to. – You'd better get your act together otherwise there won't be any tickets left.

_____

2. Match the German idiom on the left with the appropriate English idiom on the right.

1. *wie warme Semmeln weggehen*	a)	to be a thorn in s.o.'s side
2. *mir raucht der Kopf*	b)	to kill two birds with one stone
3. *in aller Munde sein*	c)	to sell like hot cakes
4. *jdm. ein Dorn im Auge sein*	d)	to be fed up (to the back teeth)
5. *ins Fettnäpfchen treten*	e)	to be on everybody's lips
6. *die Nase voll haben*	f)	my head is spinning
7. *zwei Fliegen mit einer Klappe schlagen*	g)	to let the cat out of the bag
8. *die Katze aus dem Sack lassen*	h)	to put one's foot in it

Remember, many idioms are fixed expressions – so you cannot usually change the word order or replace words at will. Grammatical changes are also not possible although you may change the tense of the verb.

Some idioms can be varied slightly. For instance if you want to say that someone has been very lucky in a difficult situation, you can either say "he fell on his feet" or "he landed on his feet". If you want to talk about happy things you did in the past, you can either say "I took a trip (*or* stroll *or* walk) down memory lane.". However, unless a different possibility is clearly marked, do not change any of the words and learn the expression as a whole unit. If in doubt, look it up in your dictionary.

Idioms are an integral part of the English language and in widespread use. They are found in all kinds of English, both formal and informal. But not all British idioms are understood by Americans or Australians and vice versa.

You will often encounter idioms in newspapers and hear them when people are talking. But beware, while many idioms have remained a fixed part of the English language, others come and go out of fashion quite quickly. So it is sometimes difficult to know which ones you can use. If in doubt, use a simpler expression – it is better to be simple and correct, than to try to use an idiom which is either out-of-date or used incorrectly.

In the "Topics" chapters you will find specific idioms to do with the individual topics. On the next few pages you will find some useful idioms that you can use to talk about many different topics.

Here are some common informal idioms that use parts of the body. Complete the idiom on the left with the right noun from the box. Then match it to the correct meaning.

lips	hands	nose	hair	head	feet	arm
brain	tongue	thumb	heels	neck	mind	

1. to breathe down s.o.'s _____

a) to begin to feel comfortable with s.th.

2. to be _____ over _____

b) to pay a lot of money

3. to be on everyone's _____

c) to watch s.o. closely

4. to let one's _____ down

d) to be sold to s.o. else

5. to find one's _____

e) to be widely talked about

6. to pay through the _____

f) to not react to s.th. (verbally)

7. to stick out like a sore _____

g) to persuade s.o. to do s.th. he or she does not really want to do

8. to change _____

h) to stand out from everything else around it

9. to bite one's _____

i) to relax and enjoy o.s.

10. to have s.th. on the _____

j) to not be able to stop talking or thinking about s.th.

11. to be a load off s.o.'s _____

k) to be deeply in love

12. to twist s.o.'s _____

l) to know you no longer have to worry about s.th.

General idioms

Here are some general idioms that will help you to structure your ideas and put forward arguments. You will often hear them when talking with native speakers or reading texts in English. When you come across them, always look at how they are used and in what context.

Useful idioms for structuring thoughts and arguments

On the one hand, I'd like to earn more money. **On the other hand**, I don't want to work longer hours.
Sometimes, the first part of the expression ("on the one hand") is left out, especially in spoken English.

to show two opposite facts or arguments

Nuclear power is the cleanest way to produce electricity. **On the other side of the coin**, some people are concerned about the safety issues involved.

used after an argument to introduce a different point of view

She has to work really long hours. **Be that as it may**, she knew that would be the case when she accepted the job.

used after arguments to show that although they might be true, you do not change your opinion

This article discusses the **pros and cons** of school uniform.

arguments for and against

For better or worse, e-commerce is now a fact of life.
This expression is often used in connection with marriage as it is part of the marriage vows.

whether one likes it or not

The economy looks good **in the short term**.
also **in the medium / long term**

for a short period of time

At the end of the day, we have to decide what is more important – freedom of choice or a ban on smoking to protect people's health.

introduces an important idea, usu. towards the climax or conclusion

Fill in the gaps in the text with a suitable idiom from the list on the opposite page. In some cases, there might be two possibilities.

1. The death penalty is a very controversial issue in the US and there are many _____.

2. _____, pro-gun activists say that the right to bear arms is laid down in the Constitution.

   _____, advocates for gun control argue that the only function of a gun is to kill.

3. New legislation to protect the environment is extremely important but _____ it's up to every individual to take responsibility.

4. Studies have concluded that the use of mobile phones is safe _____ but scientists say we also need to look at their effects _____.

   _____, it is considered safer to limit one's phone usage.

5. Many people believe that animal testing is unacceptable because it causes suffering and does not show whether a drug will harm humans. _____, some scientists argue that it can eliminate some potential drugs as being ineffective or too dangerous to test on human beings.

6. The government announced further changes in the education system today – whether _____ remains to be seen.

Useful idioms for discussing topics

The events of last week **paled into insignificance** compared with those of yesterday.
also **to fade into insignificance**

to seem unimportant when compared to s.th. else

The press often **blow** things **out of proportion**.

to make s.th. much more important than it really is

We should not **lose sight of the fact** that many people need help filling in these forms.

to forget s.th. important

The person who committed this crime must **be brought to account**.
also **to be called to account**

to be forced to explain one's actions and usually be punished for them

The investigation **shed light on** suspected terrorist activities.

to make s.th. clearer

New evidence has recently **been brought to light**.
"to bring to light" is usually used in the passive, also **to come to light**

to discover facts, often about s.th. bad

Advertising is part of life but we should **draw the line at** targeting children.
also **to draw the line at doing s.th.**

to decide not to do s.th. because one thinks it is wrong

There is a **thin line** between genius and madness.
also **fine line**

two things are very similar but the second thing is bad and the first thing is not

Journalists sometimes **cross the line** when they intrude on people's grief.

to do s.th. that is wrong or socially unacceptable

Bear in mind that she does not speak very good English when you meet her – so speak slowly.
also **to keep in mind**

to remember s.th., especially when making a decision or thinking about s.th.

Make the most of the warm weather – it's due to rain on Friday.

to take advantage of s.th. because it may not last long

Web 2.0 seems to be **the shape of things to come**.

what we have to expect in the future

We **are on the threshold of** exciting new discoveries in space.

s.th. is likely to happen very soon

Fill in the gaps in the text with a suitable idiom from the list on the opposite page. In some cases, there might be two possibilities.

1. Gun activists claim that the number of guns used for criminal

   purposes _____ when compared with

   the number that are owned and used responsibly. Furthermore,

   pro-gun activists claim that we often _____

   the fact that most crimes are committed using weapons that have

   been obtained illegally. In addition we should also _____

   _____ that guns can easily end up in the hands

   of children and cause accidents. As well as stricter controls on

   the sale of weapons they demand that people who sell guns

   without carrying the necessary checks must be _____

   _____.

2. We _____ of exciting new medical

   developments. Many scientists agree that stem cell research

   _____, offering people real hope

   of treating illnesses like diabetes and Alzheimer's. However, it is

   surrounded by controversy as some people say there is a

   _____ between producing embryonic

   stem cells in a laboratory and perfecting the cloning of humans.

   They are worried that if scientists are allowed to do the former

   they might _____ without anyone

   noticing.

Idioms that can be used in discussions

These idioms are more informal and are used in spoken English.

I'm afraid you're **missing the point**! I don't disagree with the idea, just the way he said it.	*to not understand what s.o. is trying to say*
That's **beside the point**! We're talking about how to solve the problem and not about whose mistake it was.	*not important or relevant to what is being said*
She always **speaks her mind** – even if it upsets people!	*to honestly say what one thinks*
We're **going round in circles** – I think it's time we made a decision. *also* **to go around in circles**	*to not make any progress because you keep returning to the same problem which you cannot solve*
When I heard what she had done I was **lost for words**.	*to not know what to say*
Jana is Swedish – sorry that was **a slip of the tongue** – I mean Swiss.	*to say the wrong word by accident*
I can't remember the name of the song but it's **on the tip of my tongue**.	*to know s.th. but not be able to remember it at the time, usu. a name, word, etc.*
He talked so much that I could**n't get a word in edgeways**. *usually used with "not"*	*to not be able to say anything because the person you are talking to is talking all the time*
That name **rings a bell**.	*to sound familiar*
I'm **having second thoughts about** going on holiday with her.	*to change your opinion or begin to have doubts about a decision*
I can't remember what I was going to say – I've lost my **train of thought**.	*a series of connected thoughts or ideas*

I WISH I HAD MORE HAIR. — DON'T BE A SILLY BILLY. YOU'VE GOT PLENTY OF HAIR. — HERE'S YOUR BALD, I MEAN, YOUR BOILED EGG.

Which idiom does this cartoon illustrate?

Decide which expression best fits the context.

1. As I was saying, I think we should ... er ... um ... Sorry, _____.
   a) I've lost my train of thought   b) you've missed the point

2. What was the name of the company? It's _____.
   a) on the tip of my tongue   b) a slip of the tongue

3. Let's vote on it otherwise we're not going to reach a decision. At
   the moment we're just _____.
   a) missing the point   b) going round in circles

4. Her name _____ but I'm not sure where we've met before.
   a) is a slip of the tongue   b) rings a bell

5. He hasn't understood what we were saying – he _____.
   a) has missed the point   b) has spoken his mind

6. Did I say Lisbon? I meant London – it was just _____.
   a) a slip of the tongue   b) beside the point

7. Thank you all so much for this beautiful present. I don't know
   what to say – I'm _____.
   a) going round in circles   b) lost for words

8. James is very open, he always _____.
   a) speaks his mind   b) has second thoughts

9. She seems to be _____ about accepting the job – she's not
   really sure she wants to work in marketing.
   a) missing the point   b) having second thoughts

Euphemisms

Euphemisms are words or expressions that are used to soften reality, especially when talking about something which might be found unpleasant or frightening (war, death, illness) or embarrassing (bodily functions, sex). For example, in the case of war there are many euphemisms for the word "war" itself, such as "conflict", "engagement", "armed confrontation", etc.

As a result of political correctness, new expressions have emerged to minimize offence to different racial, political and cultural groups or individuals. For instance, someone who is "visually challenged" or "visually impaired" is blind. The word "challenged" has become part of a whole group of euphemisms, e.g. "the physically challenged" are people with physical disabilities (also called "differently-abled") and "the intellectually challenged" are those with learning difficulties.

Political leaders and company executives frequently use euphemisms to make their messages seem less threatening or to put events in a better light. For example, companies talk about "downsizing" or "restructuring" rather than "firing people" and accountants might report "negative cash flow" rather than "loss of money".

Euphemisms are used to make things seem more important or to elevate someone's status, for instance you might see "administrative assistant" (secretary) or "domestic assistant" (cleaner).

A few common euphemisms

Bodily functions
You will hear many different expressions for the word toilet, including "bathroom", "little boys'/girls' room" *(informal)*, "john" *(AE, informal)*, "restroom" *(AE)*, "public convenience" *(BE)*, "WC". The best one to use is "bathroom" – it is neutral and suits most situations.

Death
Death is still a taboo subject which is why there are so many euphemisms to describe it. Some of the most common include, "to pass away", "to pass on", "to be taken", "to meet one's end" and "to meet one's maker". If you wish to pass on your condolences to somebody for their loss, you should say "I am sorry to hear that xxx has passed on / away.". Or simply "I am sorry for your loss.".

"Hello Simpson, somebody said you had gone into
the timber and phosphorus business."

Informal expressions for death which you might hear but should not actively use to avoid causing offence include "to pop one's clogs", "to kick the bucket", "to bite the dust" and "to push up the daisies". They are often also used in a humorous way.

Sex
There are numerous euphemisms for this topic, a few of the more common ones being "to sleep with someone", "to make love" and "to spend the night with someone".

And last but not least
If you are talking to a native speaker and they tell you that something is "**interesting**", be careful! Listen to the tone of voice it is said in, as English natives often use this as a euphemism for "boring" or "uninteresting" when they want to be polite.

Using euphemisms

While it is important that you can recognize and understand some of the more common euphemisms, as a general rule, it is better to avoid using them. In certain social situations, you might use them so as not to offend someone, especially if you are talking to a recently bereaved person or about bodily functions. It is kinder to say, "I was so sorry to hear your father passed away." rather than "I was so sorry to hear your father died.". Likewise, if you do not know someone well, it is considered politer (especially in the US) to ask where the "bathroom" is, rather than the "toilet". However, even in these cases, your manner of speaking and general tone is more important than whether you use a euphemism or not.

Avoid euphemisms in written English. You should aim to get your message across as clearly and truthfully as possible – hard facts are better than euphemisms, which often make arguments vaguer and less forceful.

When you read newspapers or literature in English, keep an eye open for euphemisms – they are used frequently and change fairly often. Think about why they are being used and always try to think of a plain equivalent.

What do the following euphemisms mean? Find the matching phrase in the box

> retreated – pregnant – used – bald – drug addicts – lying –
> support a woman's right to have an abortion – in prison –
> policeman – go to the toilet – a thief – unemployed –
> number of deaths – bombing attack – their own side

1. She is sometimes <u>rather economical with the truth</u>.

2. Steve has started selling <u>pre-owned</u> cars.

3. He's <u>between jobs</u> at the moment.

4. She's <u>expecting</u>.

5. The army <u>made a strategic movement to the rear</u>.

6. Mary is currently spending time <u>at a correctional facility</u>.

7. My father's getting rather <u>thin on top</u>.

8. Two soldiers were shot by <u>friendly fire</u>.

9. The latest <u>air strike</u> hit a bus station, bringing the <u>body count</u> to twenty four this month.

10. He has decided to become a <u>law enforcement officer</u>.

11. The number of <u>substance abusers</u> has increased over the past twenty years.

12. My English friend said, "I need to <u>powder my nose</u>". What did she mean?

13. I'm <u>pro-choice</u>. What about you?

14. You need to watch him, he's <u>light-fingered</u>.

Register

Different situations call for different types of register or language. Whether you choose formal or informal language or slang will depend on:

- the situation (an e-mail to a friend will sound different to a business letter)
- the person (would you talk to a friend using the same language as to your parents or a potential employer?)
- the topic (a poem is written in a different style to an advertisement or a magazine article)

In your mother tongue, you adjust automatically. It is a little more difficult in a foreign language because you have not grown up with it, but you can still develop a feeling for what is appropriate. You should always remember the following:

- If in doubt, it is better to be more formal so that people think you are polite, rather than to use slang and cause offence.
- Using informal expressions will not necessarily impress people, especially if you use them incorrectly!
- If you are uncertain whether a word is informal or not, look it up in a dictionary. After certain words you will find an indication as to what type of words they are *(formal, informal, slang,* etc.). You will also find regional labels *(US, Australia).*
- Listen to what kind of vocabulary and expressions the person you are talking to uses.

Formal language

In spoken English you use more formal language if you want to show respect to someone or to be more polite, e.g. in an interview. This is especially important in English as there is no formal pronoun "Sie". Formality and respect are shown by intonation and by using appropriate expressions. Imagine you are talking to a policeman. What would be the most appropriate way to address him in English?

- ❑ "Come here!"
- ❑ "Come here, please!"
- ❑ "Would you come here, please?"

> In English-speaking countries people very often call each other by their first names. This is very common at work; people often address their boss by his or her first name. It does not, however, mean that they are generally very informal with each other.

1. Say whether you think each of the following sentences is informal, formal or neutral.

1. What's that bloke doing over there?

2. Excuse me, please. Can you tell me where the bus stop is?

3. May I remind you that smoking is not permitted?

4. Why on earth did you do that?

5. Have you seen whatshername again? You know, the girl we chatted with at the party last week?

6. There are four exits on the aeroplane. Each one is clearly marked with the word "exit".

7. I should be most grateful if you would send me a reply as soon as possible.

2. Read the following sentences and say which one would be more appropriate in each situation.

1. Your new boss at a job interview:
   a) "What about starting next month?"
   b) "Would you be able to start next month?"

2. Two good friends talking to each other:
   a) "Why don't we go and grab a bite to eat tonight?"
   b) "Shall I make a dinner reservation for tonight?"

3. In a business letter:
   a) Dear Sir, I want to know more about the job ad in the paper.
   b) Dear Sir, I would be interested in receiving more information about the job advertised in the newspaper.

4. In an essay:
   a) I think we should get rid of the death penalty.
   b) In my opinion the death penalty should be abolished.

5. A boy talking to a girl he has just met:
   a) "Would you like to go to the cinema tomorrow night?"
   b) "I would be delighted to escort you to the cinema tomorrow."

In written English formal language is used for official matters, e.g. for business letters, essays, academic papers as well as formal speeches. When you go to an English-speaking country, you will also notice that official signs and notices are written in formal English, for example:

Shoplifters will be prosecuted	No admission to unaccompanied minors

However, non-official signs, especially in the US, are often written using abbreviations like these:

Rooms 4 rent	Drive thru	Coffee 2 go

These abbreviations mean that the signs are informal.

When you are writing in a formal style avoid the following:
- **non-specific words**, e.g. "get", "thing". Try to use a more formal alternative.
- **contractions**, e.g. "don't", "isn't". Write them out in full instead.
- **abbreviated words**, e.g. "ad", "TV". These should also be written out in full.
- **beginning sentences with the following words**, you should use the more formal equivalent instead:

but	→ nevertheless, however
and	→ in addition
or	→ alternatively
so	→ consequently, hence
also	→ in addition

- **ending a sentence with a preposition**, e.g. in informal English you will often hear, "Who did you send the letter to?". However, you should write, "To whom did you send the letter?".
- **split infinitives:** "He began to slowly realize his mistake.". In this sentence you will see that "slowly" has been inserted in between "to" and "realize". This is known as a split infinitive. It is much better to write "He slowly began to realize his mistake.".
- **expressions and fillers** such as "mind you", "by the way", "you know", "I mean", etc. You will hear them in spoken English but they should be avoided in writing.
- **phrasal verbs that can be replaced with a single verb equivalent** (also see study point "phrasal verbs" p. 146), e.g.

  to look at something → to examine something
  to come across something → to find something
- **informal idiomatic expressions and clichés**

1. You will often read the following on signs. Match the words in the box to the underlined words in each of the sentences.

> to buy – drink – to ask – entry – theatre / hall – to move –
> to get on – person under the age of 18 – to present o.s. –
> to get off – to not do – to be sorry

1. We <u>regret</u> that we cannot serve alcoholic <u>beverages</u> to <u>minors</u>.

   to regret _____   beverage _____   minor _____

2. Do not <u>alight</u> while the bus is <u>in motion</u>.

   to alight _____   to be in motion _____

3. Tickets must be <u>purchased</u> before <u>boarding</u> the train.

   to purchase _____   to board _____

4. Kindly <u>refrain from</u> smoking in the <u>auditorium</u>.

   to refrain from _____   auditorium _____

5. No <u>admittance</u>.   admittance _____

6. All visitors are <u>requested</u> to <u>report</u> to the front desk.

   to request _____   to report _____

2. Find another word for "get" in each of these sentences.

1. Could you get _____ me a knife, please?

2. I got _____ the measles over the New Year.

3. I got _____ interested in karate last year.

4. I don't get _____ why that's funny!

5. Did you get _____ any post today?

6. We got to _____ the station at six o'clock.

7. The police managed to get _____ the burglar.

8. He got _____ her to help him.

Informal language

Although we mostly use informal language when we speak, e.g. with friends and family, it is also used in written English. You will find it in headlines in the popular press, as well as in articles.

Look at this sentence from an article in *The Sun* on 16.02.07:

"A middle-aged woman who nabbed over 200 rolls of toilet paper from public loos without spending a penny has been flushed out by council staff."

Which words and expressions are informal and what would have been more neutral equivalents?

Informal English often contains idioms and phrasal verbs which make the language more colourful (you will find more information on these topics in the relevant study points). Sentences also tend to be shorter and simpler.

If you listen to native speakers, you will notice that they often use fillers such as "well", "ok", "er". Certain words such as "pretty" (in the sense of "quite", e.g. "she's pretty upset"), "dead" (in the sense of "extremely", e.g. "he's dead tired") are used frequently and should only be used in an informal context.

Abbreviations

Abbreviating words will often make them more informal, for example "lab" is more informal than "laboratory". Although it is not a problem to use the abbreviation in spoken English, it is much better to use the complete word in a written context.

Today abbreviations are used a great deal in e-mails, chat rooms and in text messages. If you are writing to a friend, it is not a problem to use them but they should only be used in an informal context. If you are communicating on a more formal level, always use the full expression. The same basic rules apply to English text message abbreviations as they do to German. Punctuation is generally omitted, as are some words. Certain words or syllables are represented by letters and numbers that sound the same.

Here are some examples:

bbl = be back later	lol = laughing out loud
tlk2ul8r = talk to you later	gr8 = great

1. Each of the following sentences contains an informal word or expression. Find a more neutral equivalent for each of them.

1. <u>Do you fancy coming out</u> _____ for a drink?

2. Can you tell me where the <u>loo</u> _____ is, please?

3. How many <u>kids</u> _____ do you have?

4. What's <u>on the box</u> _____ tonight?

5. Have you met Tim's <u>other half</u> _____ yet?

6. They had a terrible <u>row</u> _____ last night and are now not speaking to each other.

7. You're <u>nuts</u> _____ – you can't be serious!

8. I've just been jogging and I'm really <u>knackered</u> _____.

2. What do these abbreviations mean? Write them out in full.

1. c u l8r

_____

2. I 4got 2 fon u

_____

3. Pls snd Jane's no asap

_____

4. Ill b there b4 6

_____

5. Where r u? Im w8ing 4 u outside

_____

Contractions

Contractions are short forms of other words that people use when speaking and are especially common in American English. You will often hear them in films. Here are some examples:

gonna → going to   lemme → let me   kinda → kind of

Although you might see them in dialogues or in comic strips, you should never use them in any formal context.

Slang

The term "slang" refers to very informal words or phrases which are often invented by certain groups in society to create their own identity. Only those who use the right words really belong to the group. This is one of the reasons why it is so difficult for non-natives to understand and use slang correctly. Often a new meaning is created for an old word, e.g. in 2000 "wicked" also meant "cool".

> Research was carried out in 2000 on the language used by British students. The researchers actually compiled a glossary to help parents understand the words! They included "brassic" (out of money), "snag" (sausage) and "lush" (cool).

Some slang expressions have become more integrated into everyday speech, "quid" (£), "booze" (alcohol), "aggro" (short for "aggravation" and means "trouble"). Whilst it is helpful to understand them if a non-native speaker tries to use them, it can sound very unnatural. Slang expressions often also date quite quickly and "in" expressions can become "out" overnight.

Never forget that some slang expressions might cause offence to certain people. So, although it is good to understand certain words and phrases, it is better to avoid using them yourself.

Taboo words

Certain words are taboo, i.e. they are very likely to cause offence to people. These words include racist expressions, sexist language, obscene expressions and swear words. Although you might use the latter in German, it is not good to use them in English. In the US, in particular, even milder swear words are frowned upon, especially ones with a religious connotation. There are other ways of expressing yourself. The same applies to obscene gestures such as sticking two fingers up at someone.

Here are some informal expressions that you might hear. Match the neutral words in the box to the underlined expression below.

> Thanks – Stop it – It's true – Don't misunderstand me –
> I don't know – You're mad – Don't make fun of me –
> What a shame – That's not important – Have a good day –
> I don't mind – not important

1. Bye. <u>Have a good one</u>!

2. Exams are actually <u>no big deal</u>.

3. You won the lottery and you're still working? <u>You're nuts!</u>

4. She just got up and walked out. <u>No kidding!</u>

5. <u>Don't get me wrong</u>, I think he's really nice.

6. I went to the same school as her.
   <u>So what!</u>

7. <u>Knock it off!</u> I'm trying to sleep.

8. Who invented the telephone?
   <u>Search me!</u>

9. He fell over just before he reached the finishing line.
   <u>What a bummer!</u>

10. Would you like tea or coffee?
    <u>I'm easy</u>.

11. <u>Don't take the piss</u>, it's not funny!

12. Here's your food.
    <u>Cheers!</u>

Spoken English

One of the most important points about speaking a foreign language is to keep it simple! It is much more important to communicate with someone than to try to impress them with fancy words and phrases (especially if you do not use them all correctly).

Another important point is to listen carefully to what is being said. You should not be so worried about being able to communicate that you forget to do this. If you listen carefully, it will help you to understand what is being said. Although you might be nervous if you let others express their opinions, not only will the discussion be more interesting but it will also give you time to think of your answer!

Paraphrasing
When people speak a foreign language, they often get into difficulties if they cannot think of a word. As you know, this can also happen in your own language. In cases such as these, we often replace the forgotten word with a vague one and then paraphrase. Look at this sentence – what word is missing?
>"I can't find the thingy you use to unlock the door."

In Britain, people also often use words such as "thingumejig", "thingumebob" and "whatsit" if they have forgotten the word for something. If they have forgotten a person's name, they sometimes use "whatshisname" to refer to a man and "whatshername" for a woman, e.g. "Did you see whatshisname today? – He was in the office just before you left.".

These words are very informal – so take care if you use them. Remember, if you cannot think of a specific word in English, don't be afraid to paraphrase – it will help you to get through difficult situations more easily.

Asking someone to repeat something
If you want someone to repeat something, you can always say "Could you say that again, please?". British people might use the idiomatic phrase "I'm sorry. I didn't quite catch that." (meaning "please repeat") or "What was that (again)?" (more informal). It is considered impolite to merely say "What?". The expression "Pardon?" is never out of place. However, do not confuse this with the expression "pardon me" which you will often hear in the US. This means "I'm sorry". Americans often say "Excuse me?" if they want you to repeat something.

Study points

Twelve words have been paraphrased and are hidden in this grid. They run from either left to right, right to left, from top to bottom, bottom to top, or diagonally. Find them!

A	P	B	V	Q	T	R	E	F	E	O	L	M	F	G
Z	N	E	N	I	C	I	D	E	M	R	A	Q	Y	B
R	A	U	N	H	E	N	C	U	H	I	K	F	C	D
R	E	S	H	S	F	N	Y	L	S	E	M	H	A	E
N	U	M	J	Q	I	D	T	W	Y	T	R	E	F	A
X	T	L	Y	L	U	O	C	R	A	R	H	L	T	D
R	Z	N	E	S	X	E	N	E	U	G	I	I	E	L
O	S	B	A	R	F	N	D	B	B	N	X	C	R	I
T	M	C	E	F	M	A	E	D	J	R	B	O	S	N
A	D	O	L	E	S	C	E	N	C	E	I	P	N	E
T	V	M	H	P	N	I	B	M	W	E	Y	T	U	T
C	R	E	B	H	I	R	R	H	A	U	T	E	O	S
E	I	D	L	L	E	R	F	C	I	T	I	R	C	N
P	O	Y	A	K	T	U	Z	W	E	Q	N	P	C	Y
S	W	D	J	V	B	H	O	T	D	I	P	H	G	S

1. A specific date or time by which something has to be finished.

2. It helps you to draw straight lines.

3. What a person from Britain is called.

4. It flies in the sky and has big blades that go round.

5. What you call the period of change when a young person grows up.

6. What you call a person who watches a sporting event.

7. This is what you call the words of a song.

8. What you call a person who writes reviews of films, plays or concerts.

9. What you call a play which is funny.

10. The money you get when you have retired.

11. A storm with a violent wind.

12. What a doctor prescribes when someone is ill.

Conversational responses

In English there are many set phrases and expressions which people often use without thinking. It is useful to know what the correct response is. If someone introduces themselves with the rather formal expression "**How do you do?**", the correct response is "**How do you do?**". It is a set expression with a set response. Likewise, if someone says "**Pleased to meet you!**", the correct response is "**Pleased to meet you, too!**".

If someone you do not know very well asks you "**How are you?**", it is used more as a greeting. If so, it is more usual to reply "**Fine.**" or "**Fine, and you?**" than to start telling the person how you really feel in detail. In the US you will often find that waiters and shop assistants ask you "**How are you doing?**". You can either say "**Fine.**" or nothing at all.

If someone asks "**Would you mind** if I ... (opened the window / smoked / etc.)", the correct response is "**Not at all. Go ahead.**" or "**Not at all. Please do.**". Of course if you do mind, you can say "**I'd rather you didn't.**". If someone says "thank you" to you for doing something, the correct reply is "**You're welcome.**". However, do not overuse this phrase, otherwise it will sound rather over the top!

Saying numbers

British people usually call the mathematical figure "0" "**nought**" [nɔːt], e.g. "What's five times **nought**?". Americans generally call it "**zero**".

If a series of numbers is given (e.g. a telephone number, bank account number), it is often called "**oh**" like the letter "o", e.g. "My telephone number is three six oh seven five oh.". It is also pronounced "**oh**" in dates and times, e.g. "1906" (nineteen **oh** six), "9.08" (nine **oh** eight).

In measurements (such as temperatures), the British also say "**zero**", e.g. "It's extremely cold today – it's five degrees below **zero**.".

If the score is "5-0" in a team game, British people say it is "five **nil**", Americans say "five **zero**". Exceptions to this rule are tennis, table tennis, squash and badminton – the word "**love**" is used, e.g. "The score is forty **love**." (40-0).

Remember, in English a decimal point is used (not a comma), e.g. "0.5" (in *BE* spoken **nought point five**, in *AE* **zero point five**). A comma is used to separate the thousands from the hundreds in a large number. Unlike in German, in British English "**and**" is used before the last two numbers in a large number, e.g. "4,765 – four thousand seven hundred **and** sixty-five". In American English "and" is not generally used.

Similar to German, you can also say "**twelve hundred**" rather than "one thousand two hundred", although this is only done with round numbers and ones between 1,100 and 1,900.

1. Match the correct response with each of these sentences.

1. Thank you so much for all your help.	a) Oh, you shouldn't have! Thank you.
2. Can I get you anything?	b) I'm so sorry.
3. Make yourself at home!	c) Not at all. Don't mention it.
4. I've brought you some flowers.	d) Congratulations!
5. My grandma died last week.	e) Bless you!
6. someone sneezes	f) Just a coffee, please!
7. We won the match!	g) Thanks, I'll need it!
8. Best of luck!	h) That's very kind. Thank you.

2. Read the following sentences and decide how the number "0" should be pronounced in each case (following the British English rules).

love	oh	nil	nought	zero

1. What's the score? – It's 2-0 _____ to England.

2. My account number is 563 240 _____.

3. How many "0" _____ are there in one million?

4. Water freezes at 0 _____ degrees.

5. The next train leaves at 12.04 _____.

6. Five minus five is 0 _____.

7. Inflation rose 0.5% _____ in September.

8. My mobile number is 0172 ... _____.

9. 40 – 0 _____; Henman to serve.

10. The first Nobel Prizes were awarded in 1901 _____.

Everyday expressions that are useful in conversations

Informal expressions are marked with an asterisk.

As I was saying, …
This brings the conversation back to the topic in question.

Come to think of it*, she said she'd be here by now.

If you ask me*, she's …
This is an informal way of saying "in my opinion".

Talking of films, why don't we go to the cinema tomorrow night?

That reminds me, I haven't got back to him yet.
You can use this expression if you remember something after hearing something that someone else has said.

Mind you, that's not what she told me.
This is used to introduce an afterthought.

Anyway, I think it's time for me to be on my way now.
This word is often used when the speaker thinks the subject or conversation is closed.

The thing is*, I didn't have time to go there as I was already late.
This expression introduces a topic or an excuse.

Hang on!* / **Hold on!*** / **Wait a minute***
These expressions are used to stop someone interrupting. The first two are very informal. "Hold on" can also be used when you are on the telephone and you want someone to wait a moment while you do something or get someone, e.g. "Hold on – I'll just check that for you!". However, it is very informal. If you are talking to someone you do not know well, it is better to say "Just a moment, please and I'll check that for you.".

(Now) let me see, …
You can use this expression if you need to gain time to think about something.

Read the following sentences and decide which answer is the correct one in each case.

1. _____, it's about time for me to go now –
   my train is leaving soon.
   a) Anyway   b) Mind you   c) Now let me see

2. _____, can I finish what I was saying?
   a) Hang on   b) That reminds me   c) The thing is
   _____, I think it would be better to do
   that after the Christmas holidays.
   d) Now let me see   e) As I was saying   f) Mind you

3. Jane's off sick today. _____, she didn't
   want to have to do the test!
   a) If you ask me   b) Now let me see   c) Wait a minute
   _____, she'll only have to take it next
   week if she's not here today.
   d) As I was saying e) Mind you   f) Anyway
   _____ tests, how did you do in the maths
   test last week?
   g) That reminds me h) If you ask me   i) Talking of

4. _____, what are we going to do today?
   a) Now let me see   b) Wait a minute   c) If you ask me

Useful phrases for discussions

One of the most important things to remember is to remain polite, even if the discussion is a little heated. If you are chairing the discussion, you need to ensure that everyone remains calm and that no one monopolizes the discussion. Here are some phrases that will help you to get your meaning or point across – even in difficult situations – without causing offence. Remember, your tone of voice will also determine whether you sound polite or not!

Disagreeing politely
If you don't mind me saying ...
That's true up to a point but ...

Interrupting politely
May I interrupt you there for a moment, please?
Excuse me for interrupting, but ...

Dealing with being interrupted
May I finish what I was saying, please?
I haven't quite finished what I was saying.

Defending yourself
I don't think you actually got my meaning ...
I'm afraid there seems to have been a misunderstanding. I actually said that ...

Responding to a suggestion
That's a good idea!
I think we should look into this a little further before we make our final decision.
Before we make our decision, I think we should consider the following ...

Returning to the original subject
We seem to have got sidetracked. Let's get back to the point.
As I was saying before ...

Stopping someone monopolizing a discussion
Thank you very much. Would anyone else like to add anything?
I'm sorry to interrupt you but I'm afraid you'll have to stop there.

When you give a presentation or talk, it is important to structure what you are saying to keep the audience's attention. There are set phrases in English that you can use at different points in your talk which act as signposts to your audience.
Number the following phrases in the order in which they could be used in a talk or presentation.

a) I'd now like to sum up the main points which were ...   ____

b) Good morning ladies and gentlemen.   ____

c) I'll now be happy to answer your questions.   ____

d) The main points I will be talking about are ...   ____

e) Now I'd like to turn to something completely different.   ____

f) I'd like to illustrate this first point with ...   ____

g) The topic of my presentation today is ...   ____

h) In conclusion, let me leave you with this thought ...   ____

i) I'd like to start by outlining ...   ____

"I sort of thought your presentation was going to be in powerpoint."

Improving your English

Using synonyms

As in all languages, in English there are also words which are often overused. Nothing is more boring than reading or hearing "he said" or "nice" all the time. When you are writing an essay or giving a speech or presentation, it is important to vary the words you are using to make what you are saying more interesting. However, do make sure that you use the other words correctly (they might be followed by a different preposition or take an object, etc.)! It is better to have three alternatives that you can use correctly than five or six that you do not feel sure about.

A thesaurus will help you to find alternatives. But remember that the words listed do not all have exactly the same meaning and they are not all used in the same way. Review all the options (look them up in a dictionary to find out their exact meaning if necessary) and then choose the one that fits best.

When you are writing, you first have to think about what you really mean. For example, if you are talking about a film you have seen, instead of saying it was "**interesting**", think about *why* it was interesting:

Was it a thriller?	→ gripping
Did it make you think?	→ thought-provoking
Was it a love story?	→ romantic
Did it make you laugh?	→ amusing / entertaining
Did the story interest you?	→ fascinating
Did it present the subject in a new way?	→ refreshing
Did it change your attitude?	→ motivating / inspiring

Did you "**like**" the film? Or did you "enjoy" it or even "love" it? You could be more precise – maybe you "admired" the acting or perhaps you "appreciated" the special effects.

Another phrase that should be added to your blacklist is "a lot of" – be more specific! Here are a few alternatives:

Followed by a countable noun	Followed by an uncountable noun
Countless people	Vast amounts of money
A great many people	A good / great deal of money
A considerable number of people	A considerable amount of money
A large number of people	A large amount of money

Note "amount" should only be followed by an uncountable noun!

1. Put the correct word in the gaps in each of these sentences.

1. I had a **nice** _____ time at Jane's party last night –
   her friends are really **nice** _____ and the food was
   nice _____, too.
   delicious   *enjoyable*   *great*

2. We had a really **bad** _____ journey! Jim is a
   really **bad** _____ driver and we almost had a **bad**
   _____ accident.
   serious   *poor*   *terrible*

3. I thought the play was really **good** _____, didn't
   you? –
   Yes, I did. The actors were **good** _____, too.
   But it was also a **good** _____ audience.
   superb   *talented*   *appreciative*

2. Each of the words on the left has two near synonyms on the right. Find them!

1. dirty	a) exorbitant
	b) immaculate
2. expensive	c) reasonable
	d) absurd
3. big	e) squalid
	f) vast
4. cheap	g) ridiculous
	h) pricey
5. silly	i) spotless
	j) massive
6. small	k) minute [maɪˈnjuːt]
	l) filthy
7. clean	m) inexpensive
	n) tiny

185

The word "**very**" is also often overused and there are a great many alternatives. If you can learn to use these correctly, you will improve your style. However, you have to be careful when you use some of them because they only collocate with specific words. You will have to learn these as set expressions. Generally speaking, alternatives such as "exceedingly", "extremely" or "incredibly" can be used with most gradable adjectives, i.e. ones which have a comparative or superlative form such as "hot", "tired" and "good".

Be careful when using the adverbs "absolutely", "completely", "totally" and "utterly" (the latter is a little more formal). These are used to qualify adjectives that are *all or nothing*, such as "destroyed", "exhausted", "bankrupt" (a person is either bankrupt or not – they cannot be "very bankrupt"). You might hear these adverbs being used with gradable adjectives. However, you should avoid doing so.

"Highly" is used with "competitive", "controversial", "effective", "paid", "recommended", "respected", "successful" and "(un)likely". If in doubt, use one of the more general alternatives such as "extremely". "Deeply" is mainly used with words to do with feelings, e.g. "ashamed", "concerned", "religious", "shocked", "upset". "Strongly" is a useful adverb for essay writing. It collocates with verbs, especially ones to do with opinions, such as "to believe", "to deny", "to disagree", "to feel", "to influence", "to oppose" and "to suggest".

Although you might hear the informal synonym "dead", e.g. "that was dead boring", you should not use it in written English.

Another informal adverb of degree that you will often hear is "**pretty**" *(ziemlich)*. Try using "rather", "somewhat" and "fairly" instead.

COMPUTER SALES

"This is a pretty sophisticated PC, sir. Do you
have a child at home who can help?"

186

1. Decide which adverb is correct in each of these sentences.

1. The building was _____ (completely / incredibly) destroyed in the fire.

2. She was _____ (exceedingly / utterly) exhausted.

3. He was _____ (extremely / totally) worried when he heard the news.

4. You're _____ (incredibly / utterly) wrong!

5. This book is _____ (absolutely / incredibly) boring.

6. He's _____ (extremely / totally) clever, isn't he?

2. Choose an adverb from the opposite page to complete each of these sentences.

1. I am _____ concerned about your health – you really need to go and see a doctor.

2. He's _____ competitive, isn't he?

3. I'm afraid, I _____ disagree with this decision. I think it is _____ unlikely that the others will agree to it either.

4. He was _____ ashamed of his behaviour at the party.

5. She is a _____ respected member of the community.

6. His parents are _____ religious.

7. Many Americans _____ believe in the right to bear arms.

8. I was _____ shocked when I heard about the accident.

As ~~said~~ **mentioned** at the beginning of this study point, you should also try to find alternatives for the verb "**to say**". Look at how the following sentence can be made more specific:

"She **said** that she was hungry.",
→ She **admitted** / **confessed** that she was hungry. *(zugeben)*
→ She **announced** that she was hungry. *(ankündigen)*
  Be careful with the spelling of "to announce" (it is often misspelt by native speakers!).
→ She **claimed** that she was hungry. *(behaupten)*
→ She **declared** that she was hungry. *(verkünden)*
→ She **explained** that she was hungry. *(erklären)*
→ She **remarked** that she was hungry. *(äußern)*

Be honest, what would you rather read, "said" or one of the above?

"I must _____,
Johnson is a hell of a salesman."
Think of an appropriate verb to complete this cartoon.

The same is true of the verb "**to tell**". Look at how the following sentence can be changed (but be careful, because some of these verbs need an object!):

"He **told me to** be careful.",
→ He **mentioned** that I should be careful. *(erwähnen)*
→ He **suggested** that I should be careful. *(vorschlagen)*
→ He **informed** <u>me</u> that I should be careful. *(jdn. informieren)*
→ He **advised** <u>me to be</u> careful. *(jdn. raten / empfehlen etw. zu tun)*
→ He **reminded** <u>me to be</u> careful. / He **reminded** <u>me</u> that I should be careful *(jdn. an etw. erinnern)*

The meaning is different in each case – so once again, you have to decide what you are really trying to say.

1. **The following verbs can be used instead of the verb "to ask", depending on what is meant. First of all, match each one to its German equivalent. Then use each verb to complete one of the sentences.**

   1. to enquire* about s.th.   a) *etw. verlangen*
   2. to enquire* after s.o.   b) *jdn. inständig bitten, etw. zu tun*
   3. to request s.th.   c) *sich nach etw. erkundigen*
   4. to demand s.th.   d) *sich nach jdm. erkundigen*
   5. to beg s.o. to do s.th.   f) *um etw. bitten*

   * This is more common in *BE*. In *AE* "inquire" is more common.

1. She _____ his father.

2. Visitors are kindly _____ not to walk on the grass.

3. The public _____ an explanation from the government.

4. He _____ her not to leave him alone.

5. They _____ the price of the car.

2. **Replace the verb "to say" or "to tell" in these sentences.**

1. Should doctors **tell** _____ people about possible side effects when they prescribe medicines?

2. At the meeting he **said** _____ that he was leaving.

3. Her doctor **told** _____ her to give up smoking.

4. She **told** _____ her parents again that she was going swimming after school.

5. I must **say** _____, I haven't read that book yet.

Useful expressions for writing

When you are writing a speech, presentation or essay, it is very important to vary the language to make it more interesting for your audience or reader. The "Idioms" study point lists some general idioms that are helpful. In this section, you will find some verbs and expressions to improve your style. Only a few examples have been given in each case – it is better to learn a few and use them correctly. Even so, do not use all of these expressions in one essay, otherwise it will end up sounding unnatural and rather like a list of phrases. Finally, remember to always learn the complete expression (take special note of the preposition!) so that you are able to use it correctly.

General tips
When you are writing an essay or speech, try to avoid using the word "**problem**" all the time, e.g. "This essay deals with the **problem** of global warming.". You could also use "issue" (see p. 55), "question", "topic" or "subject". If you want to talk about a particular part of a problem or issue, use the word "aspect", e.g. "Increased trade is only one aspect of globalization.".

Also remember to use alternatives for "**I think**", such as "I believe", "I am convinced", "in my opinion", "in my view" or "as far as I am concerned". And do not forget, if you want to qualify a verb of feeling such as "to believe", you can use the adverb "strongly" (see page 186).

Useful collocations
Here are a few useful expressions to help you to set out your ideas more clearly. As they are set collocations, make sure you do not change them.

"We must also take the causes of global warming into consideration."
The expression does not have to be separated, you can also say "to take into consideration the causes of global warming".

"I will draw a distinction between the effects of globalization in developing and developed countries."
This expression is used to show a difference between two things. You can also say "to make a distinction between".

"Recent reports have provided new insights into the use of lethal injection as a means of administering the death penalty and have also raised important questions about the death penalty in general."
You can also say "to raise an important question" or use the adjective "interesting" instead of "important".

Paraphrasing
Sometimes you might need to paraphrase something to clarify it. To do so, you can use expressions such as "**in other words**", "**that is to say**" (this is more formal) or simply "**that is**", e.g. "Recent estimates suggest that over 337 million people speak English as their first language and around 350 million speak it as their second language. **In other words**, it is one of the most widely used languages in the world.".

Giving examples
Examples are given "**to illustrate**" or "**to show**" a point. You can always introduce an example using familiar expressions such as "**for example**" or "**for instance**". However, you could vary this with an expression such as "**The following example shows …**", "**This can be illustrated / shown by …**" or simply "**A good example is …**". Look at these two sentences:
"This example **illustrates** what global changes we are facing today."
"Supporters of globalization argue that it has raised living standards in developing countries. This **can be illustrated by** the story of the Indian farmer who …"
After you have given an example you might want to comment on it, saying it is a "**perfect example of s.th.**" or a "**clear illustration of s.th.**".

Introducing studies and quotations
If you are using data contained in studies or statistics, verbs such as "**to show**", "**to demonstrate**", "**to indicate**" or "**to prove**" are helpful, e.g. "A recent study **demonstrated** the need for more information to be given to pupils to help them make informed choices.".

When you are introducing a quotation, you can use a simple verb such as "**to suggest**", "**to believe**", "**to state**", "**to claim**", e.g. "In his film *An Inconvenient Truth*, Al Gore **states that** 'Scientists have an independent obligation to respect and present the truth as they see it'."

If you agree with the author's statement, you can either put the adverb "correctly" in front of the verb, or introduce your quotation with one of these phrases, "**to draw (s.o.'s) attention to s.th.**", "**to point s.th. out**", "**to make s.th. clear**", e.g. "In his film *An Inconvenient Truth*, Al Gore **points out that / correctly states that** 'Scientists have an independent obligation to respect and present the truth as they see it'."
If you disagree, then you can put the adverb "**mistakenly**" before the verb.

191

Showing cause and effect

Imagine you are writing an essay about the growing problem of obesity *(Fettleibigkeit)*. You might want to explain what has caused it and what effects it is having. If you are talking about the main causes, then use verbs such as "**to be responsible for s.th.**", "**to be the cause of s.th.**", "**to give rise to s.th.**" or "**to provoke s.th.**". Take a look at the following examples:

"The latest report **gave rise to** a great deal of criticism."

"Behavioural and environmental factors are **responsible for** the growing problem of obesity."

You might want to mention other things that are responsible. Verbs such as "**to be a factor in s.th.**", "**to contribute to s.th.**" or "**to influence s.th.**" will enable you to do so, e.g. "A person's lifestyle – whether they do any exercise and what kind of food they eat – **greatly contributes** to the likelihood of them becoming obese.".

As you can see in the above example, the expressions can be qualified to add intensity. But be careful, because they are not all qualified using the same words e.g. "**to be an** important / central **factor in s.th.**", "**to greatly contribute to s.th.**", "**to strongly** / greatly **influence s.th.**".

Structuring and connecting your thoughts

There are many familiar phrases that you can use to structure your writing and connect your thoughts, including "**on the one hand** ...", "**firstly**", "**in addition**" and so on. However, you can also use verbs to structure your writing. Look at the following examples:

I would / should like to begin by saying that ...
This expression is commonly used in speeches or presentations.

It is often claimed / stated that genetically engineered food is not natural.

This brings me / us to the next question, that of ethics and genetic engineering.
*There are two ways of continuing this expression. Either using "**that of + noun**" (as above) or by putting a colon after the word "question" and asking the question, e.g. "This brings us to the next question: what are the ethical issues involved?". A similar expression is, "This **leads us to** the next topic.".*

"Let us now **turn our attention to** the question of ethics and genetic engineering."

"Let us now briefly **touch on the** ethical issues involved."

"I will now **address** the question of ethics and genetic engineering."

Expressing certainty or doubt
You can show that something is definite by using one of these phrases, "Without (a) doubt", "Undoubtedly" or "There can be no question / doubt that", e.g. "Better healthcare has undoubtedly led to a decrease in infant mortality.".

If something is likely, you can introduce your statement with, "It is likely / probable that" or "There are reasons to believe that" or use "In all probability", e.g. "It is likely that global warming is responsible for the recent increase in the number of hurricanes.".
"Likely" is often preceded by a qualifying word such as "very", "most" or "quite", depending on what you want to say.

If something is true in most cases, use expressions such as "generally speaking", "as a rule", "on the whole" or "In the majority of / most cases", e.g. "Generally speaking, it is wrong to lie. However, many people agree it is acceptable if it is done for a good reason.".

If you are reporting something and you do not know whether it is true or not, use adverbs such as "supposedly", "allegedly" and "apparently", e.g. "He was on trial for allegedly stealing the painting.".
The use of modal verbs such as "might", "could" and "may" and verbs such as "to seem" also help to express uncertainty.

The changing face of English

English is a very rich language – it has borrowed words from all the different languages with which it has come into contact over the centuries, including Latin, Greek, German, French, Japanese, Arabic and the Scandinavian languages. In many cases the pronunciation has been anglicized – so it is always worth checking the pronunication in a dictionary. Look at the following words – do you know from which languages they come?

kindergarten	yoghurt	budgerigar
tsar	algebra	mosquito
aubergine	caravan	pseudonym
yacht	igloo	fjord
tsunami		

English spread very quickly due to the British Empire, the economic, cultural and military importance of the US and recently due to the Internet. As Jeremy Paxman wrote in his book *The English* (London: Penguin Books, 1999, p. 234), "the greatest legacy the English have bequeathed the rest of humanity is their language [...] Three quarters of the world's mail is written in English, four fifths of all data stored on computers is in English and the language is used by two-thirds of the world's scientists.". To a large extent it has become the language of technology, science, travel and international politics. It is now estimated that a quarter of the world's population can speak some English.

A changing language

As English is now spoken by so many people in so many different contexts, new expressions are being constantly invented. This can happen in a variety of ways, including:

- joining two words together: **outsourcing** = out + sourcing
- by mixing two words and their meanings: **brunch** = breakfast + lunch
- borrowing from other languages: **karaoke** from the Japanese
- adding a prefix or suffix: <u>bio</u>diversity
- using the initials to form a word: **WiFi** = <u>wi</u>reless <u>fi</u>delity
- changing the way a word is used (conversion): **to google** (from Google™)

As many of these words are coined to describe fleeting trends, only time will tell if they become established in the English language. Nevertheless, it is always fun – also for native speakers – to try to guess their meaning.

All of these words are relatively recent additions to the English language and have been used in newspaper articles. Read these sentences and fill in the gaps using the words from the box.

> bad hair day – freegan – movieoke – snail mail –
> spin doctor – spoiler – WAGs

1. This word refers to the wives and girlfriends of footballers.

   _____

2. Information about a book, film or game that can spoil a person's enjoyment of it if they are experiencing it for the first time.

   _____

3. A person who believes in getting as much food as possible from free sources, such as food thrown away by restaurants.

   _____

4. A day when everything goes wrong and you generally also feel unattractive. _____

5. Someone who is employed by politicians (or public figures) to manipulate public opinion in their favour. _____

6. Ordinary post as opposed to e-mail. _____

7. A form of entertainment in which a person acts out a scene from a film while the film silently runs in the background.

   _____

Text messaging or texting has given rise to a whole new language of abbreviations. Many people are now very concerned about its impact on young people's writing and spelling. What do you think?
(see "Register" p. 168)

"... and I'm proficient in two languages – English and text messaging."

Gender issues

Over the past years, English has been increasingly influenced by gender issues. This means that neutral expressions are usually favoured over ones specifying a person's sex, e.g. "**sales assistant**" ("~~salesman~~"), "**flight attendant**" ("~~stewardess~~"), "**spokesperson**" ("~~spokesman~~"), sometimes "**human race**" (instead of "mankind"). "**Ms**" was introduced as a neutral alternative to "Mrs" and "Miss" (previously a woman's marital status was obvious through the use of "Mrs" rather than "Miss"). If you are writing or speaking to a woman for the first time, it is best to address her as "Ms". However, if a person introduces herself as "Mrs" or "Miss", you should follow her lead.

Gender sensitivity has led to a problem concerning the personal pronoun used with words such as "someone", "everyone", "anyone", etc. Grammatically speaking, the following sentence is incorrect, "Everyone brought their favourite music.". "Everyone" should be followed by a singular personal pronoun, this used to be "he". However, to avoid being sexist, one should use "he or she" and this results in a rather clumsy construction. In informal English you will thus frequently see the plural. In written English it is best to try to avoid it by writing the sentence in a more neutral way, e.g. "Everyone brought a favourite piece of music.".

American English

American English differs greatly from British English in pronunciation, spelling, grammar and meaning. You should not mix the two when you are writing unless you are giving a direct quotation. Here are a few of the differences in spelling that you should know.
Some words end in:

- "**-tre**" in *BE*, "**theatre**", but in "**-ter**" in *AE*, "**theater**"
- "**-our**" in *BE*, "**colour**", but in "**-or**" in *AE*, "**color**"
- "**-ogue**" in *BE*, "**dialogue**", but in "**-og**" in *AE* "**dialog**"
- Some verbs in British English can end in "**-ise**" or "**-ize**", "**to realise / to realize**", but end in "**-ize**" in *AE*, "**to realize**".
- If the final "**-l**" is an unstressed syllable, it is not usually doubled in *AE*, e.g. *AE* "**traveler**" but *BE* "**traveller**".

Sometimes Americans use a different word for the same idea, e.g. "**pavement**" *(BE)*, "**sidewalk**" *(AE)*. In some cases, the same word has a different meaning, e.g. "**pants**" are "trousers" in *AE* and "underwear" in *BE*. These differences can give rise to laughs or blank faces when Brits and Americans talk with each other.

1. Match the British English words on the left to their American equivalents on the right.

1. biscuit	a) carry-on baggage
2. bonnet (of car)	b) closet
3. boot (of car)	c) cookie
4. cooker	d) crosswalk
5. hand luggage	e) faucet
6. petrol	f) gas
7. tap	g) hood
8. vest	h) stove
9. wardrobe	i) trunk
10. zebra crossing	j) undershirt

2. Write *AE* or *BE* next to the words according to whether the spelling is American or British.

1. a) center _____ b) centre _____

2. a) speciality _____ b) specialty _____

3. a) jewellery _____ b) jewelry _____

4. a) catalog _____ b) catalogue _____

5. a) car tire _____ b) car tyre _____

6. a) to practice _____ b) to practise _____

7. a) honor _____ b) honour _____

8. a) to analyse _____ b) to analyze _____

An American went to his British friend's house for lunch. Just before it was served, the American asked his friend whether he could quickly go to the bathroom to wash up. She looked at him rather strangely and said that she had a dishwasher and that she usually did the washing-up in the kitchen. What did they both mean?

Last thoughts

Improving your English

You have probably heard it all before, but the best way to improve your English is to read English, listen to the radio, songs and podcasts in English, watch films in the original and talk to native speakers.

When you are reading, listening or talking to others, always bear in mind what kind of English is being used – i.e. is it American English or another form of English spoken by people as a first language? Or is it English by non-natives? Is it a formal or informal context? These questions are important if you want to make a note of any particular expressions or words, so that you know how to use them at a later stage.

A word about watching films in the original. Do not be disheartened if you do not understand very much at first! It can be very helpful to have the English subtitles on – especially if the characters are speaking dialect or simply very fast. You can then read what is being said and it is more challenging than having subtitles in German. Try not to stop the film too often – you do not need to understand every word, as long as you can understand the gist. The more you hear, the more you will immerse yourself in the language and the easier it will become.

English and the Internet

The Internet has opened up a great many opportunities. Not only does it enable everyone to access endless amounts of information in English but due to advances in technology, podcasts, streaming video and web radio it also provides real-time options for listening to English. In addition, you can make contact with like-minded English speakers through websites and groups and there are now many ways of communicating with each other. However, whilst this might seem very attractive, a word of warning! Just because something is written in English, does not mean it is necessarily correct. Many non-natives write in English and even native speakers make mistakes. Just because an expression is cited by Google a few thousand times does not mean you can use it blindly – it might occur on websites that are not written by natives. Always look at where the websites are located first and then, in addition, decide whether you think the source is trustworthy. If you are looking for expressions or language to use in writing, go to reliable sources such as dictionaries, official and / or authoritative websites such as government websites, those run by established organizations and large newspapers.

At the end of the day
Do not try to impress people with long words and complicated phrases – otherwise you will either sound like a thesaurus or worse, if you use them incorrectly, you will be misunderstood. This is true of both written and spoken English.

At the end of the day, the most important point to remember is that languages are about communicating and being able to express yourself.

Topics

All about people

p. 6　1. the Kennedy family
　　　2. Marilyn Monroe
　　　3. Princess Diana
　　　4. Sir Alexander Fleming
　　　5. Mother Theresa

Phrasal verbs

p. 8:	1. b	2. c	3. a
p. 14:	1. d	2. c	3. e
	4. f	5. a	6. b
p. 16:	1. b	2. c	3. a

Exercises (pp. 18-21)

1. 1. of　　2. for　3. to; from
　　4. from　5. at　6. at
　　7. in

2. the Brown family –
　die Familie Brown
　to run in the family –
　in der Familie liegen
　family ties –
　Familienbande
　extended family –
　Großfamilie
　immediate / close family –
　engste Familie
　loving family –
　liebevolle Familie
　dysfunctional family –
　gestörte Familie

3. 1. come over
　　2. come forward; pull through
　　3. ran into
　　4. going round; getting over
　　5. clear up

4. blind date –
　Verabredung mit einer / einem Unbekannten
　single person –
　Single
　failed marriage –
　gescheiterte Ehe
　confirmed bachelor –
　eingefleischter Junggeselle

5. 1. talks nineteen to the dozen –
　　　does not stop talking
　　2. let your hair down –
　　　relax and enjoy yourself
　　3. got on like a house on fire –
　　　got on extremely well
　　4. take it easy – relax and rest
　　5. has a heart of gold –
　　　is very kind and generous
　　6. have second thoughts –
　　　have serious doubts
　　7. tie the knot – get married
　　8. (I')m sick and tired –
　　　(I) have had enough
　　9. has been feeling under the
　　　weather – has been feeling
　　　unwell
　　10. (she')s been walking on air –
　　　(she')s been extremely happy

6. 1. to bite one's nails –
　　　an den Nägeln kauen
　　2. to run one's fingers through
　　　one's hair – *sich mit den
　　　Fingern durch die Haare fahren*
　　3. to drum one's fingers on the
　　　table – *mit den Fingern auf
　　　den Tisch trommeln*
　　4. to grind one's teeth –
　　　mit den Zähnen knirschen
　　5. to pick one's nose –
　　　in der Nase bohren
　　6. to clench one's fist –
　　　eine Faust machen
　　7. to furrow one's brow –
　　　die Stirn runzeln

7. 1. contract　2. pick up
　　3. develop　4. sustained / suffered
　　5. alleviate / relieve / ease
　　6. catch

Living together

p. 22: 1. Winston Churchill
　　　2. Lyndon B. Johnson
　　　3. Margaret Thatcher
　　　4. Bill Clinton

Phrasal verbs
p. 26:   1. b   2. c   3. a
p. 28:   1. d   2. a   3. b   4. e   5. c
p. 32:   1. c   2. a   3. b

Exercises (pp. 38-41)
1.   1. to   2. to; of   3. against
     4. on; of; with   5. on
     6. in   7. of / towards

2.   *The correct answers are:*
     1. politics   2. policy
     3. politics; politics; are
     4. policy   5. policy

3.   1. broke into; steal; lie low
     2. practise   3. roads; road
     4. street   5. scholar
     6. grades
     7. has laid him low
     8. Scientists   9. democratic

4.   a) to pull s.th. off
     b) to be mixed up in s.th.
     c) to make off with s.th.
     d) to sign up for s.th.
     e) to break out
     f) to stand for s.th.

5.   seeker
     migrant
     sanctuary
     asylum
     immigrant
     controls

     economic **migrant**
     to apply for **asylum**
     border **controls**
     asylum **seeker**
     to seek **sanctuary**
     illegal **immigrant**

6.   1. a   2. b   3. b   4. a   5. a
     6. b   7. b   8. a

Global issues

Phrasal verbs
p. 42:   1. d   2. c   3. a   4. b
p. 44:   1. b   2. e   3. a   4. c
         5. d
p. 46:   1. c   2. a   3. b
p. 48:   1. d   2. a   3. b   4. c
p. 52:   1. c   2. a   3. b
p. 54:   1. b   2. c   3. a
p. 56:   1. c   2. a   3. e   4. b
         5. d

p. 56:   1. Jurassic Park
         2. Artificial Intelligence
         3. Matrix

Exercises (pp. 58-61)
1.   1. on; per   2. for   3. with
     4. of   5. to; in   6. to; at
     7. in   8. in

2.   **body count** – number of people
     killed
     collateral damage – civilian
     deaths
     friendly fire – killing people on
     your own side
     soft target – unprotected target

3.   1. human   2. humanity
     3. human   4. humane
     5. humanity; humane
     6. human   7. human; human

4.   1. to break out
     2. to avert war
     3. to be rolling in it
     4. to have issues
     5. to spend money
     6. to alleviate poverty
     7. to lend money
     8. to effect

5.   1. The police pulled him over.
     2. He gave himself up.
     3. Forty years ago he came up
        with a good idea and set up his
        own business.
     4. Many plant and animal
        species are dying out
        as ...

5. We need to weigh up the pros and cons ...

6. Global warming has already brought about changes ...

6. 1. d 2. f 3. e 4. c
   5. b 6. a

1. from bad to worse
2. in the same boat
3. tighten our belts
4. the end justifies the means
5. vicious circle
6. the tip of the iceberg

Work and leisure

Phrasal verbs
p. 62: 1. c 2. a 3. b
p. 64: 1. b 2. c 3. a
p. 66: 1. b 2. a 3. c
p. 70: 1. c 2. a 3. d 4. b

Exercises (pp. 74-77)
1. 1. on 2. to 3. in 4. on
   5. on 6. In 7. in; at

2. 1. diary 2. appointment
   3. deadline 4. calendar

3. a) to stand in for s.o.
   b) to win s.o. over
   c) to stick at s.th.
   d) to chill out
   e) to come up with s.th.
   f) to look into s.th.
   g) to run into s.o.

   1. ran into; is standing in for
   2. has come up with; win over
   3. stick at

4. a) to accept a job offer
   b) to knock off work
   c) to be on sick leave
   d) to quit a job
   e) to be made redundant
   f) to go freelance
   g) to apply for a job

5. *The correct answers are:*
   1. match *(BE)*; nil 2. exercise
   3. court 4. a fund
   5. pension

6. a) feet b) neck c) ears; eyes
   d) feet

   1. am up to my ears/eyes in; is breathing down my neck
   2. have itchy feet; find your feet

7. 1. c 2. e 3. d 4. a
   5. f 6. b

Film, fashion and the media

Phrasal verbs
p. 78: 1. c 2. a 3. b
p. 80: 1. c 2. a 3. b

Exercises (pp. 88-91)
1. 1. in 2. about 3. on 4. in
   5. on; for 6. to 7. In

2. 1. come up with; go for
   2. Stand out
   3. kick off
   4. let on

3. report   coverage
   statement   page
   broadcast   item

   front **page**   eyewitness **report**
   news **item**   media **coverage**
   to issue a **statement**
   news **broadcast**

4. a) to access a website
   b) to do market research
   c) to build up a profile
   d) to launch a product
   e) to create a buzz
   f) to disclose information

5. 1. dubbed
   2. cameo role; lead / starring role
   3. critic
   4. on location

6. 1. factory
   2. to have stomach ache
   3. to avert controversy
   4. to wear formal clothes
   5. to be empty
   6. to change s.o.'s clothes

7. to be ready
8. to forget s.th.

7. 1. d   2. c   3. h   4. a
   5. g   6. e   7. f   8. b

   1. carries weight
   2. gut feeling
   3. tried and tested
   4. fashion victim
   5. the pros and cons
   6. spread the word

Literature and the arts

Phrasal verbs
p. 92:   1. c   2. a   3. b
p. 94:   1. c   2. a   3. d   4. b

Exercises (pp. 100-103)
1. 1. through   2. at   3. by
   4. In   5. along   6. out of
   7. with   8. from

2. 1. an interval   2. break
   3. pause   4. interval

3. 1. brought in   2. snapped up
   3. went to   4. dipped into;
                    get into

4. moving   gripping
   entertaining   shallow
   heavy-going
   spellbinding
   thought-provoking

5. 1. to make history –
      Geschichte schreiben
   2. to give a performance –
      eine Vorstellung geben
   3. to release an album –
      ein Album veröffentlichen
   4. to take up an instrument –
      *anfangen, ein Instrument zu
      spielen*
   5. to steal the show –
      *den anderen die Schau
      stehlen*
   6. to hold an audition –
      *jd. vorsprechen / -singen /
      -spielen lassen*

7. to make an entrance –
   auftreten

6. 1. art   2. arts   3. art   4. arts
   5. art; arts

7. 1. no expense was spared
   2. changed his tune
   3. stole the show; an up-and-
      coming
   4. hit the right note
   5. is poking fun at; it's been a
      roaring success

Study points

Easily confused words

p. 104:   past; passed

p. 105:   1. whether; weather
   2. two; to; too
   3. poor; paw
   4. they're; their; there
   5. knew; new
   6. tale; tail
   7. ate; eight
   8. brake; break
   9. bored; board
   10. heel; heal

p. 107:   1. current
   2. formerly
   3. principle
   4. minors
   5. site
   6. draft
   7. alter
   8. was praying
   9. course
   10. stationary
   11. minor

p. 109:   1. b   2. a   3. a   4. c
   5. b   6. c   7. b   8. b

p. 111:   1. contents   2. Classics
   3. dependants; besides
   4. classical   5. beside
   6. dependent   7. content

Key to the exercises

8. classic   9. content
10. classic   11. Besides

p. 113:   1. d   2. e   3. b   4. f
        5. h   6. a   7. g   8. c

p. 113: b) desert island

p. 115:   1. b   2. a   3. a   4. a
        5. b   6. b   7. b   8. a
        9. b   10. b

p. 117:   1. c   2. b   3. b   4. c
        5. a   6. a   7. a   8. c
        9. b

More easily confused words

p. 119:   1. c   2. a   3. b   4. c
        5. c   6. a   7. b   8. b

p. 121:   1. audience
        2. conscious
        3. aware
        4. spectator
        5. viewers
        6. borrow
        7. conscious
        8. onlookers
        9. lend

p. 123:   1. interval
        2. countryside
        3. deadly
        4. break
        5. Nature
        6. trip
        7. break
        8. fatal
        9. lethal
        10. pause

p. 125:   1. economy
        2. economical
        3. temperature
        4. economic
        5. ready
        6. Economics
        7. temperature
        8. finished
        9. economics

p. 127:   1. fit   2. sick   3. fit
        4. suits; matches   5. sick
        6. suit   7. the sick; ill

p. 128:   b) a shadow

p. 129:   1. c (recognized)
        2. a   3. b   4. b
        5. b (had not realized)
        6. b   7. a   8. a

False friends

p. 131:   1. a   2. b   3. b   4. b
        5. c   6. b   7. b   8. c
        9. b   10. a   11. b

p. 133:   1. topical
        2. vulgar
        3. committed
        4. critic; review; audience
        5. murderer; poison; tray
        6. pensioner; pension
        7. waistcoat

Singular or plural?

p. 135:   1. a) a;   *Paprika*
          b) –;   *Pfeffer*
        2. a) an;   *Bügeleisen*
          b) –;   *Eisen*
        3. a) a;   *Krach*
          b) –;   *Lärm*
        4. a) –;   *eine Arbeitsstelle*
          b) a;   *Werk* (hier:
                    Komposition)
        5. a) a;   *Jugendlicher*
          b) –;   *die Jugend*
        6. a) –;   *Papier*
          b) a;   *Dokument,*
                    Schriftstück
        7. a) –;   *Politik*
          b) a;   *Politik; Strategie*
        8. a) a;   *Land*
          b) –;   *Boden*
        9. a) a;   *Leben*
          b) –;   *Leben*
       10. a) –;   *Handel*
          b) a;   *Geschäft* (to do
                    a roaring trade = *ein*
                    Bombengeschäft
                    machen)

Prepositions in fixed expressions

p. 137:
1. at (great) risk
2. at all costs
3. at the age of
4. at length
5. at first sight
6. at (great) risk
7. at his suggestion
8. At the risk of
9. at her expense

p. 139:
1. For goodness sake
2. day by day
3. From then on
4. by heart
5. by chance
6. For your information
7. side by side
8. for fun
9. for a change
10. by hand
11. by yourself

p. 141:
1. in time
2. in turn
3. In addition to
4. in detail
5. in honour of
6. In actual fact
7. Off the record

p. 143:
1. on average
2. out of reach
3. on the Internet
4. to a certain extent
5. on time
6. on foot
7. out of the question; on principle
8. out of practice
9. on purpose
10. out of fashion

p. 145:
1. in; of 2. by; on
3. At 4. for
5. in 6. Under; out of
7. On 8. without
9. In; of 10. for
11. From 12. in
13. By 14. under

Phrasal verbs

p. 146: 1. e 2. d 3. a 4. b 5. c

p. 147:
1. like
2. attacked
3. tried to get
4. be attracted to
5. choose / have
6. decreased
7. sets
8. sank
9. stopped working
10. be remembered

p. 149:
1. told people she was gay
2. disappear
3. was published
4. appeared
5. implying
6. criticizing
7. reach
8. discovered

p. 151:
1. are always friends again
2. invents
3. put cosmetics on
4. finding
5. attributed
6. killed
7. entered your name in the list
8. suppressed
9. criticizes me

p. 153:
1. made him start to laugh a lot
2. cause
3. began their journey
4. made a bomb explode
5. start doing
6. started
7. shorten them
8. consume
9. fill

Idioms

p. 154: to get on very well
I want to travel

Key to the exercises

p. 155: 1. (I')ve been feeling under the weather – (I')**ve been feeling ill**
2. has been on the run – **has been trying to avoid being caught**
3. had a narrow escape – **just managed to avoid danger**
4. get your act together – **organize yourself**

   1. c   2. f   3. e
   4. a   5. h   6. d
   7. b   8. g

p. 157: 1. neck
2. head over heels
3. lips   4. hair
5. feet   6. nose
7. thumb   8. hands
9. tongue 10. brain
11. mind   12. arm

   1. c   2. k   3. e
   4. i   5. a   6. b
   7. h   8. d   9. f
  10. j   11. l   12. g

p. 159: 1. pros and cons
2. On the one hand; on the other hand
3. at the end of the day / be that as it may
4. in the short term; in the long term; Be that as it may
5. On the other side of the coin / On the other hand
6. for better or worse

p. 161: 1. pales / fades into insignificance; lose sight of; bear / keep in mind; brought / called to account
2. are on the threshold; is the shape of things to come; thin / fine line; cross the line

p. 162: a slip of the tongue

p. 163: 1. a   2. a   3. b
4. b   5. a   6. a
7. b   8. a   9. b

Euphemisms

p. 167: 1. lying
2. used
3. unemployed
4. pregnant
5. retreated
6. in prison
7. bald
8. their own side
9. bombing attack; number of deaths
10. policeman
11. drug addicts
12. go to the toilet
13. support a woman's right to have an abortion
14. a thief

Register

p. 168: 1. Would you come here, please?

p. 169: 1. informal
2. neutral
3. formal
4. informal
5. informal
6. neutral
7. formal

   1. b   2. a   3. b
   4. b   5. a

p. 171: 1. to regret – **to be sorry**; beverage – **drink**; minor – **person under the age of 18**
2. to alight – **to get off**; to be in motion – **to move**
3. to purchase – **to buy**; to board – **to get on**
4. to refrain from – **to not do**; auditorium – **theatre / hall**
5. admittance – **entry**

6. to request – **to ask**; to report – **to present o.s.**

1. fetch
2. contracted
3. became
4. understand
5. receive
6. arrived at
7. catch
8. persuaded

p. 172: **to nab** to steal – **loo** toilet – **to spend a penny** pun: "to spend a penny" = to go to the toilet and the lady did not pay for the toilet rolls – **flush** pun: "to flush the toilet" and to "flush s.o. out" (to discover s.o.)

p. 173:
1. Would you like to come out
2. toilet
3. children
4. on the television
5. partner
6. argument
7. insane / mad
8. tired / exhausted

1. see you later
2. I forgot to phone you
3. Please send Jane's number as soon as possible
4. I'll be there before 6 o'clock
5. Where are you? I'm waiting for you outside

p. 175:
1. Have a good day
2. not important
3. You're mad
4. It's true
5. Don't misunderstand me
6. That's not important
7. Stop it
8. I don't know
9. What a shame
10. I don't mind
11. Don't make fun of me
12. Thanks

Spoken English

A	P	B	V	Q	T	R	E	F	E	O	L	M	F	G
Z	N	E	N	I	C	I	D	E	M	R	A	Q	Y	B
R	A	U	N	H	E	N	C	U	H	I	K	F	C	D
R	E	S	H	S	F	N	Y	L	S	E	M	H	A	E
N	U	M	J	Q	I	D	T	W	Y	T	R	E	F	A
X	T	L	Y	L	U	O	C	R	A	R	H	L	T	D
R	Z	N	E	S	X	E	N	E	U	G	I	I	E	L
O	S	B	A	R	F	N	D	B	B	N	X	C	R	I
T	M	C	E	F	M	A	E	D	J	R	B	O	S	N
A	D	O	L	E	S	C	E	N	C	E	I	P	N	E
T	V	M	H	P	N	I	B	M	W	E	Y	T	U	T
C	R	E	B	H	I	R	R	H	A	U	T	E	O	S
E	I	D	L	L	E	R	F	C	I	T	I	R	C	N
P	O	Y	A	K	T	U	Z	W	E	Q	N	P	C	Y
S	W	D	J	V	B	H	O	T	D	I	P	H	G	S

Key to the exercises

p. 179: 1. c   2. f   3. h
4. a   5. b   6. e
7. d   8. g

1. nil   2. oh
3. noughts   4. zero
5. oh   6. nought
7. nought   8. oh
9. love   10. oh

p. 181: 1. a   2. a; e
3. a; e; i   4. a

p. 183: a) 7   b) 1   c) 9
d) 3   e) 6   f) 5
g) 2   h) 8   i) 4

Improving your English

p. 185: 1. enjoyable; great; delicious
2. terrible; poor; serious
3. superb; talented;
appreciative

1. e; l   2. a; h   3. f; j
4. c; m   5. d; g   6. k; n
7. b; i

p. 187: 1. completely
2. utterly
3. extremely
4. utterly
5. incredibly
6. extremely

1. deeply
2. highly
3. strongly; highly
4. deeply
5. highly
6. deeply
7. strongly
8. deeply

p. 188: admit

p. 189: 1. c   2. d   3. f
4. a   5. b

1. enquired after
2. requested
3. demanded

4. begged
5. enquired about

1. inform / warn
2. announced
3. advised
4. reminded
5. admit

Changing face of English

p. 194: kindergarten – *German*;
tsar – *Russian*; aubergine –
French (from Arabic);
yacht – *Dutch*; tsunami –
Japanese; yoghurt –
Turkish; algebra – *Arabic*;
caravan – *French (from
Persian)*; igloo – *Eskimo*;
budgerigar – *Aborigine*;
mosquito – *Spanish /
Portuguese*; pseudonym –
Greek; fjord – *Norwegian*

p. 195: 1. WAGs
2. spoiler
3. freegan
4. bad hair day
5. spin doctor
6. snail mail
7. movieoke

p. 197: 1. c   2. g   3. i
4. h   5. a   6. f
7. e   8. j   9. b
10. d

1. a) *AE*   b) *BE*
2. a) *BE*   b) *AE*
3. a) *BE*   b) *AE*
4. a) *AE*   b) *BE*
5. a) *AE*   b) *BE*
6. a) *AE*   b) *BE*
7. a) *AE*   b) *BE*
8. a) *BE*   b) *AE*